MERMAID
COLORING
BOOK

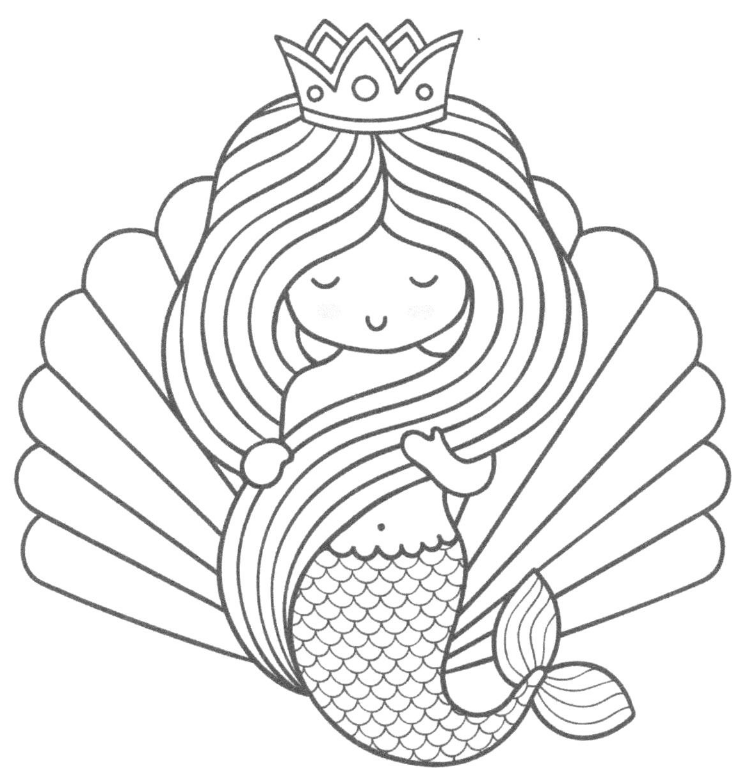

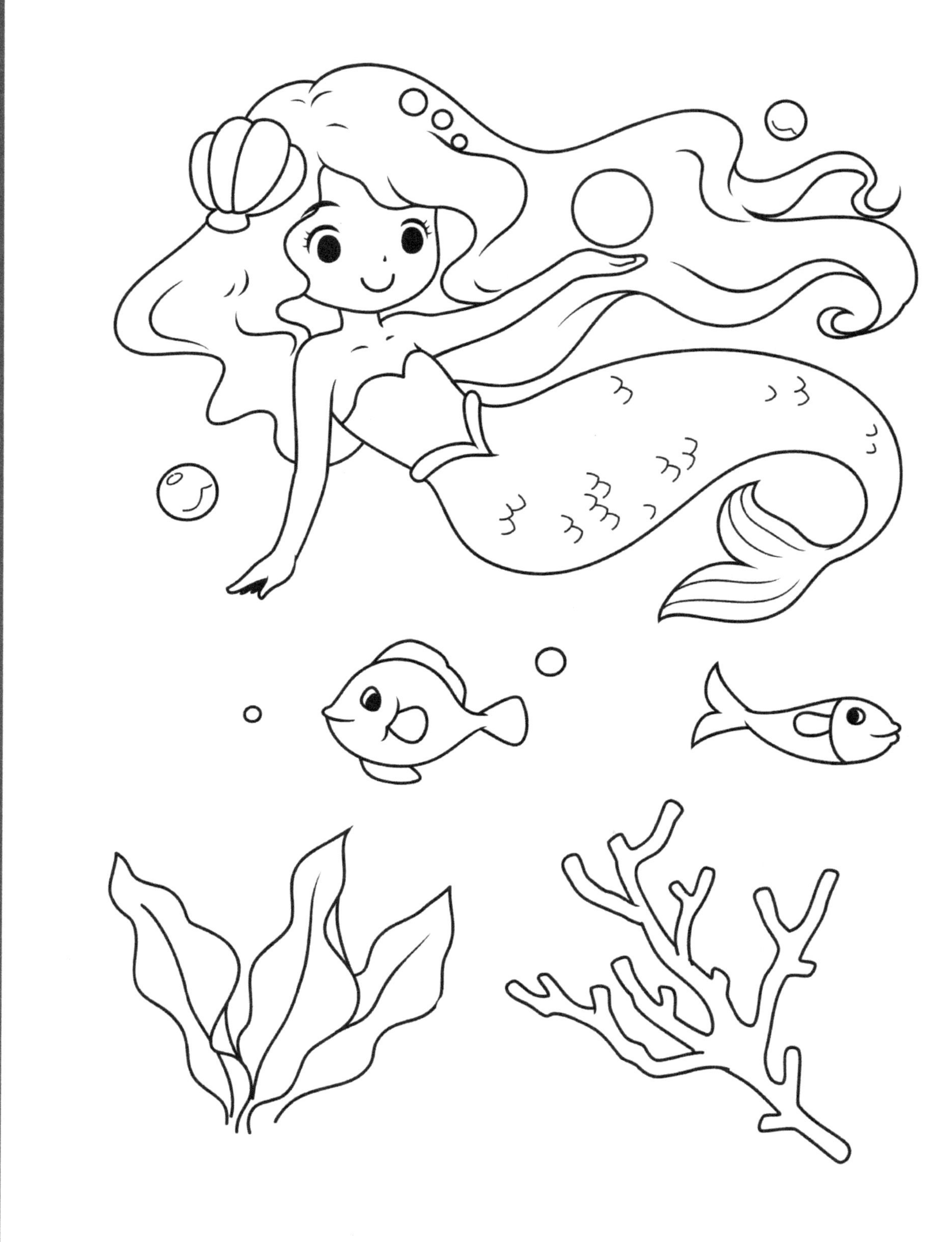

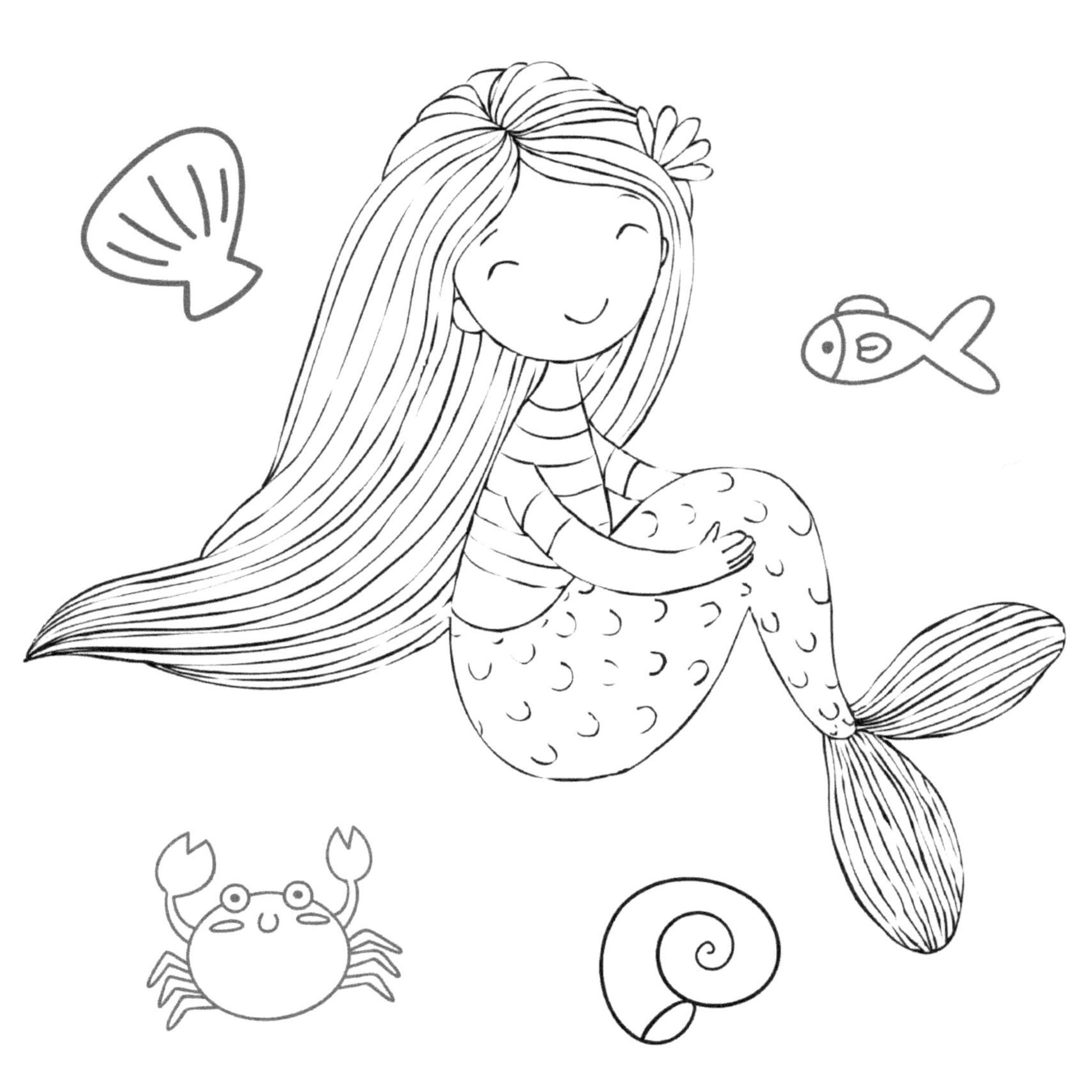

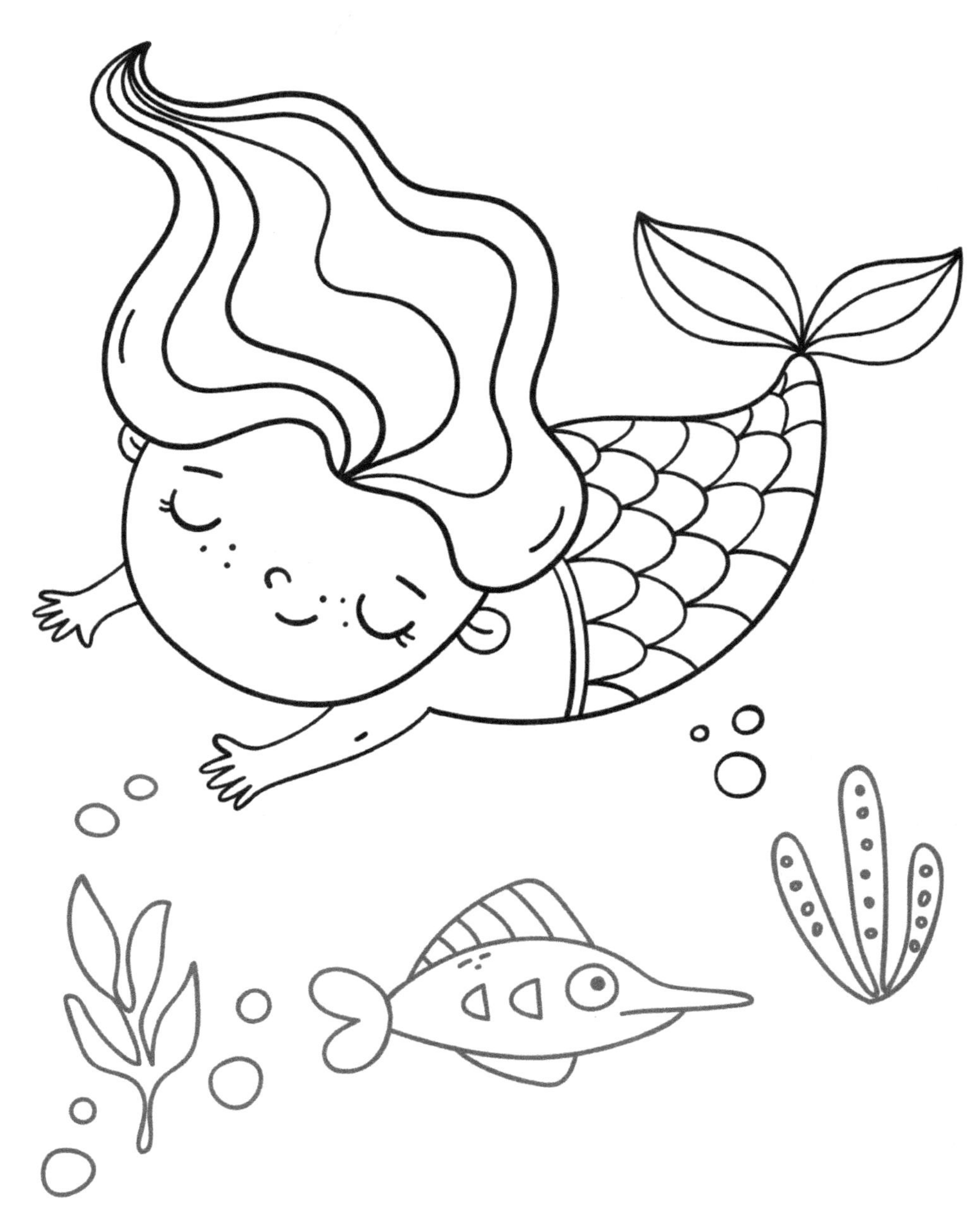

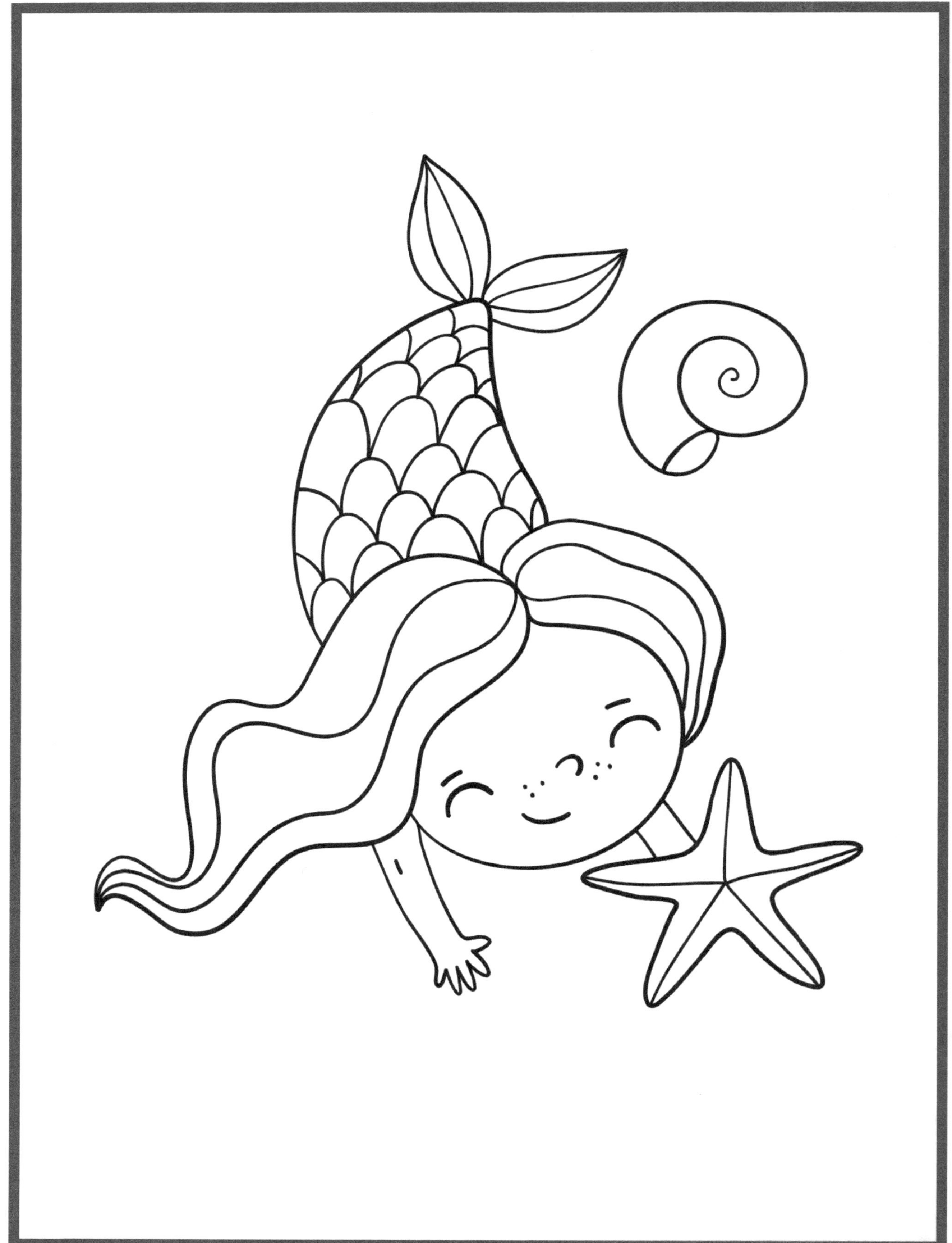

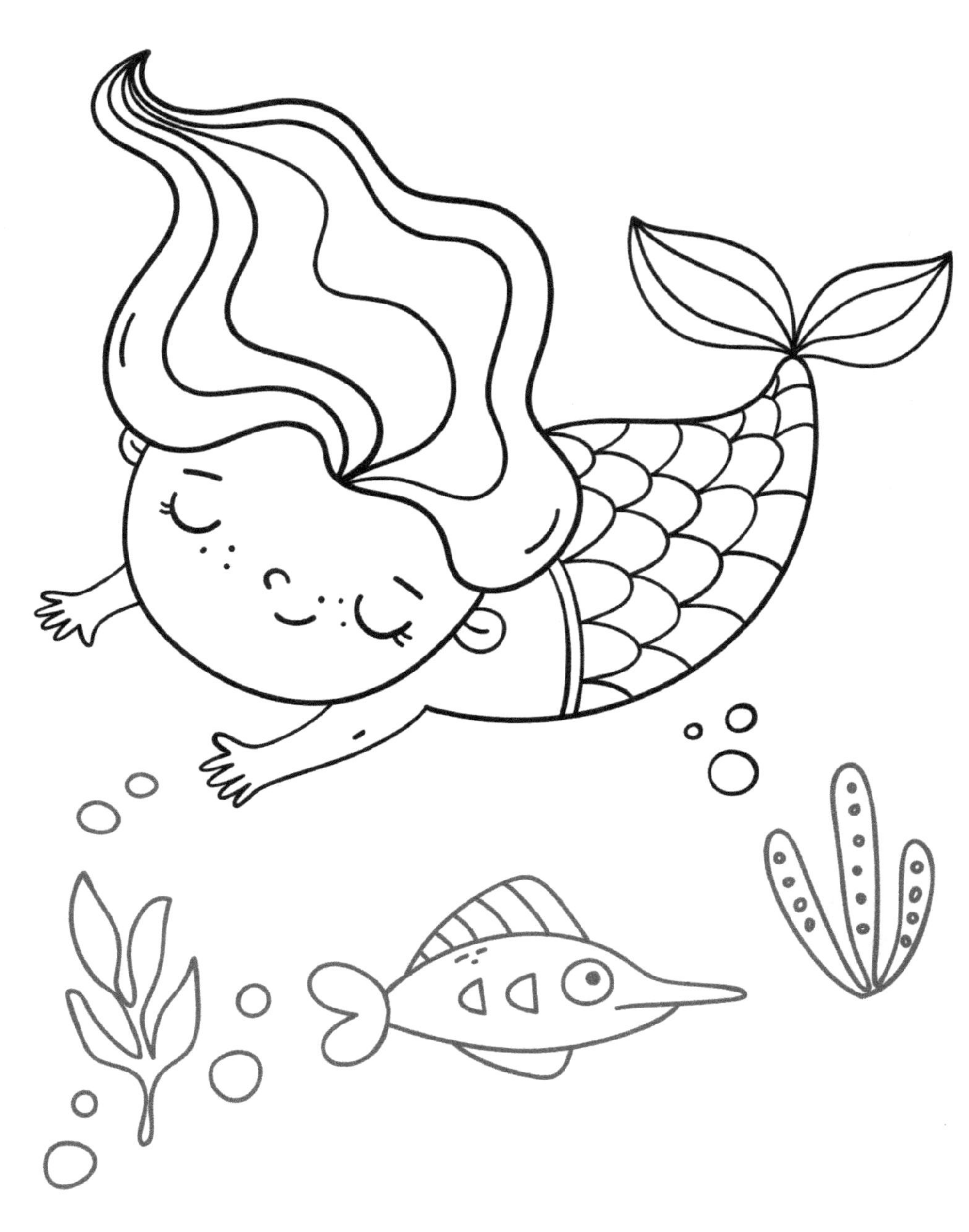

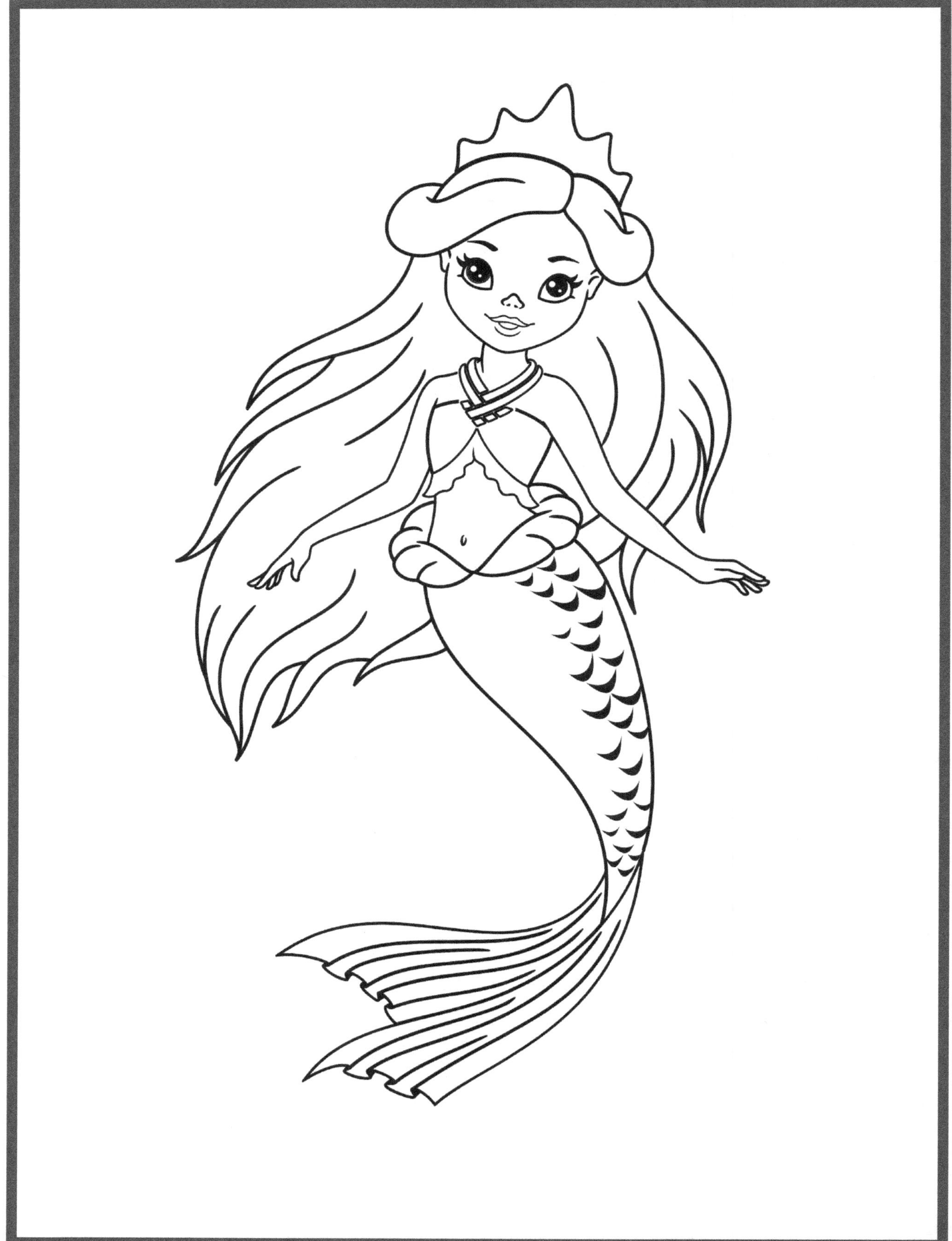

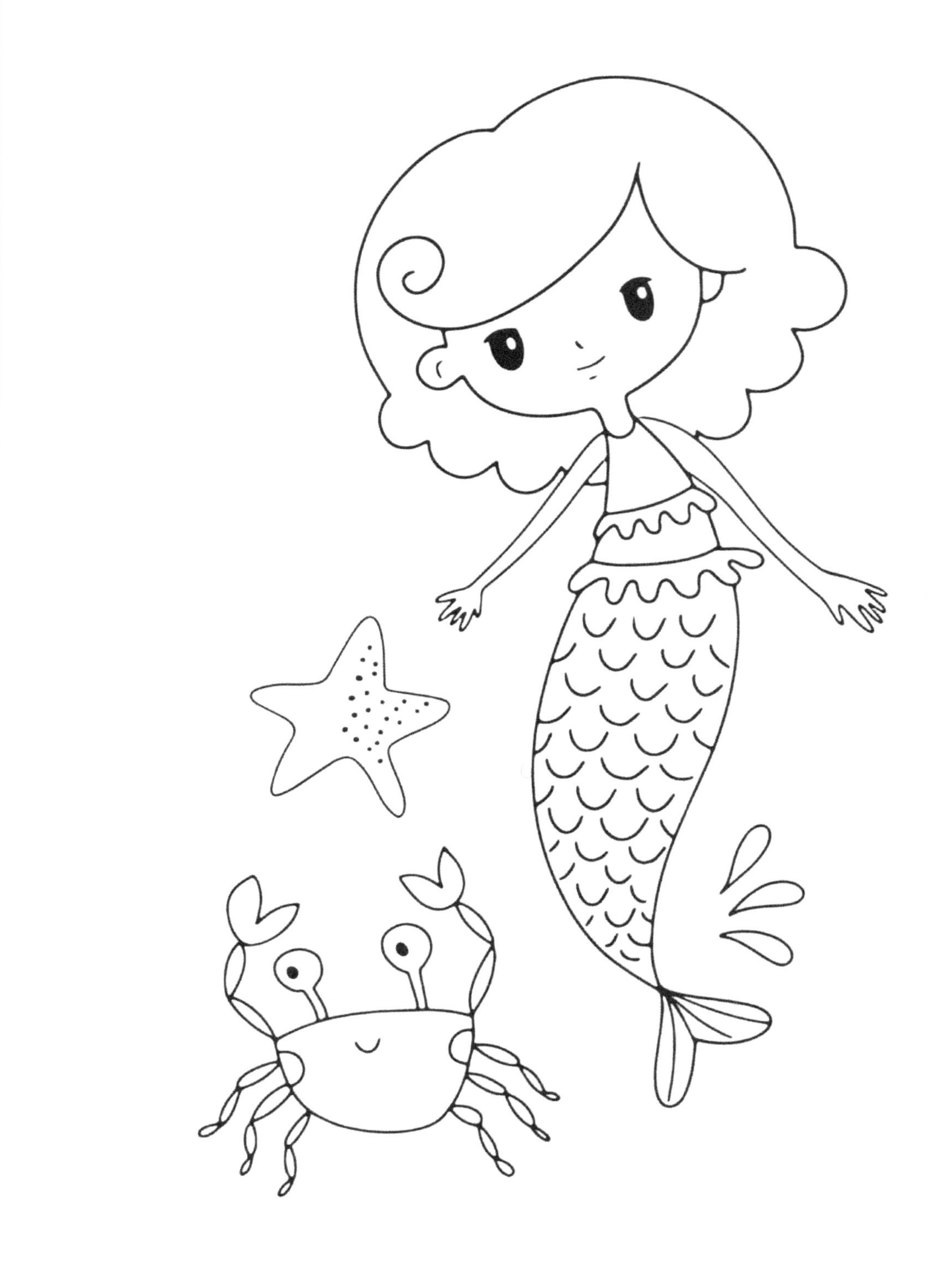

Beach party

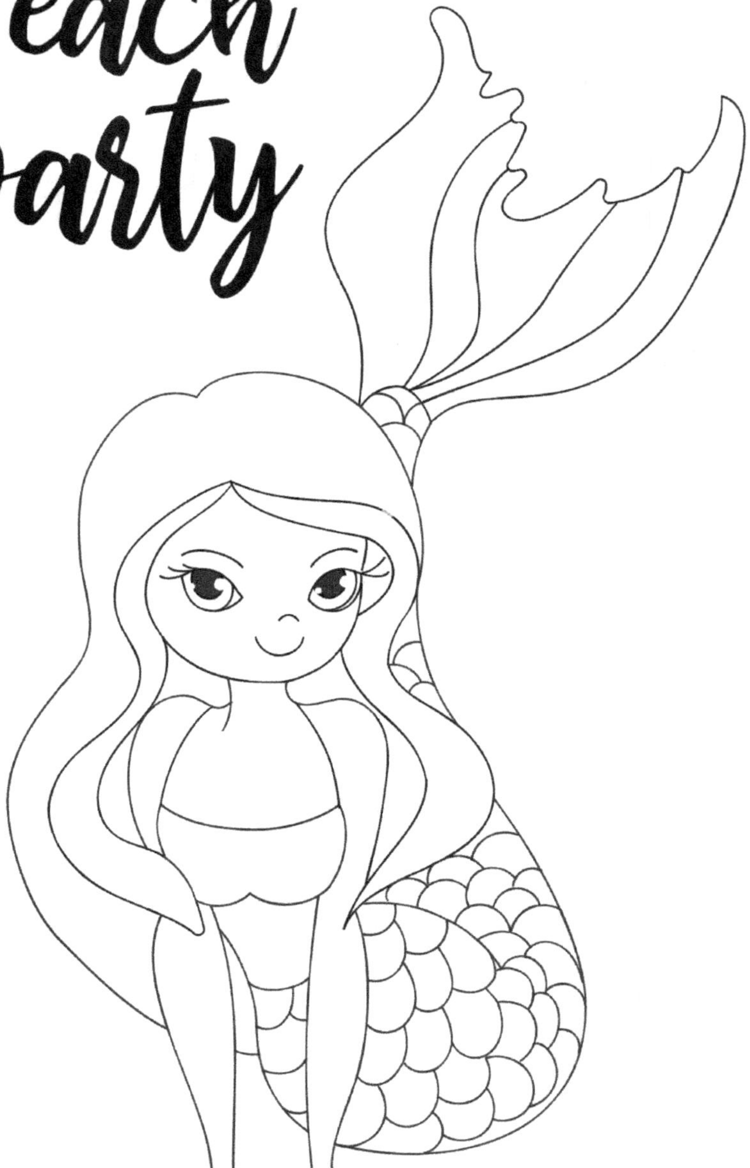

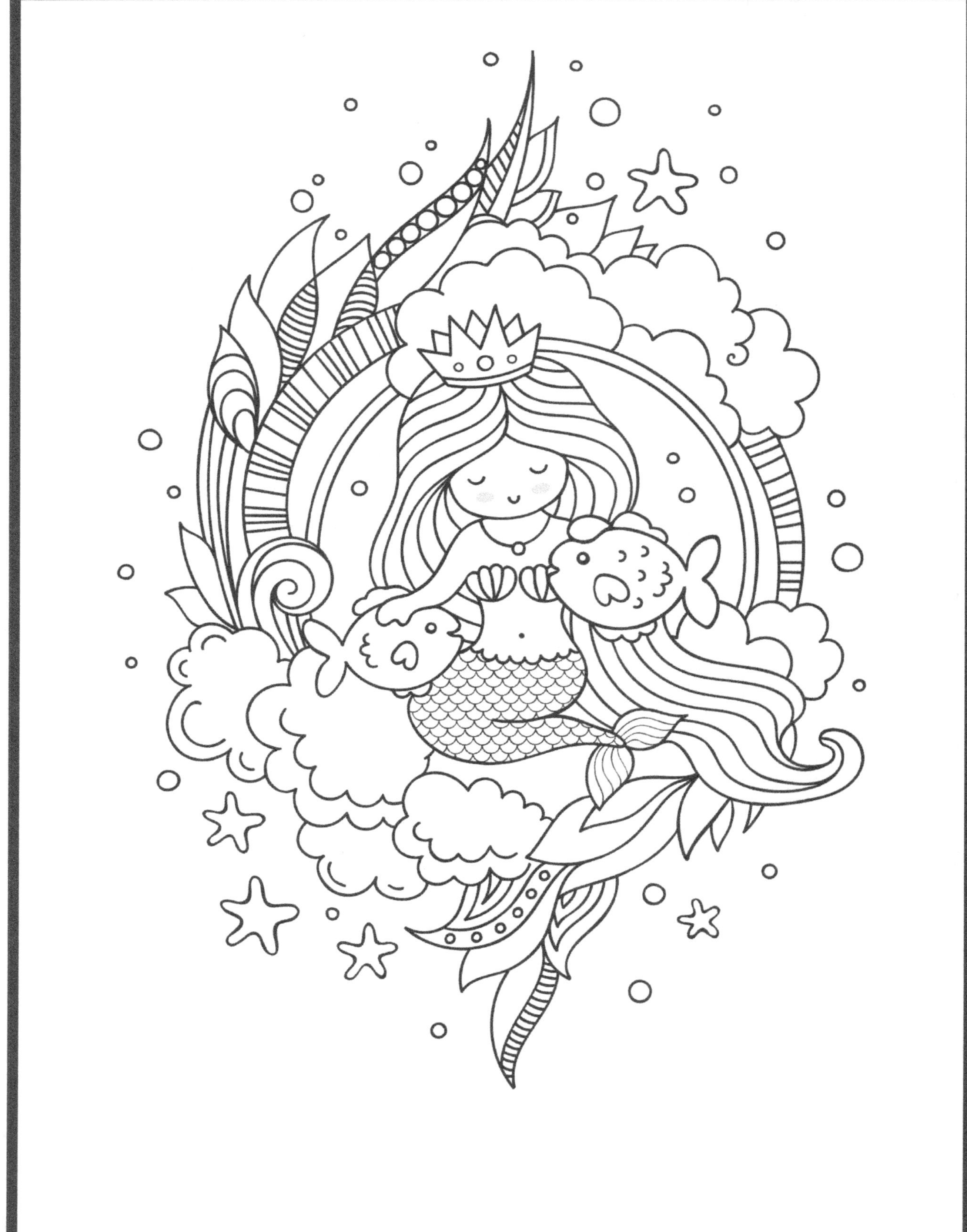

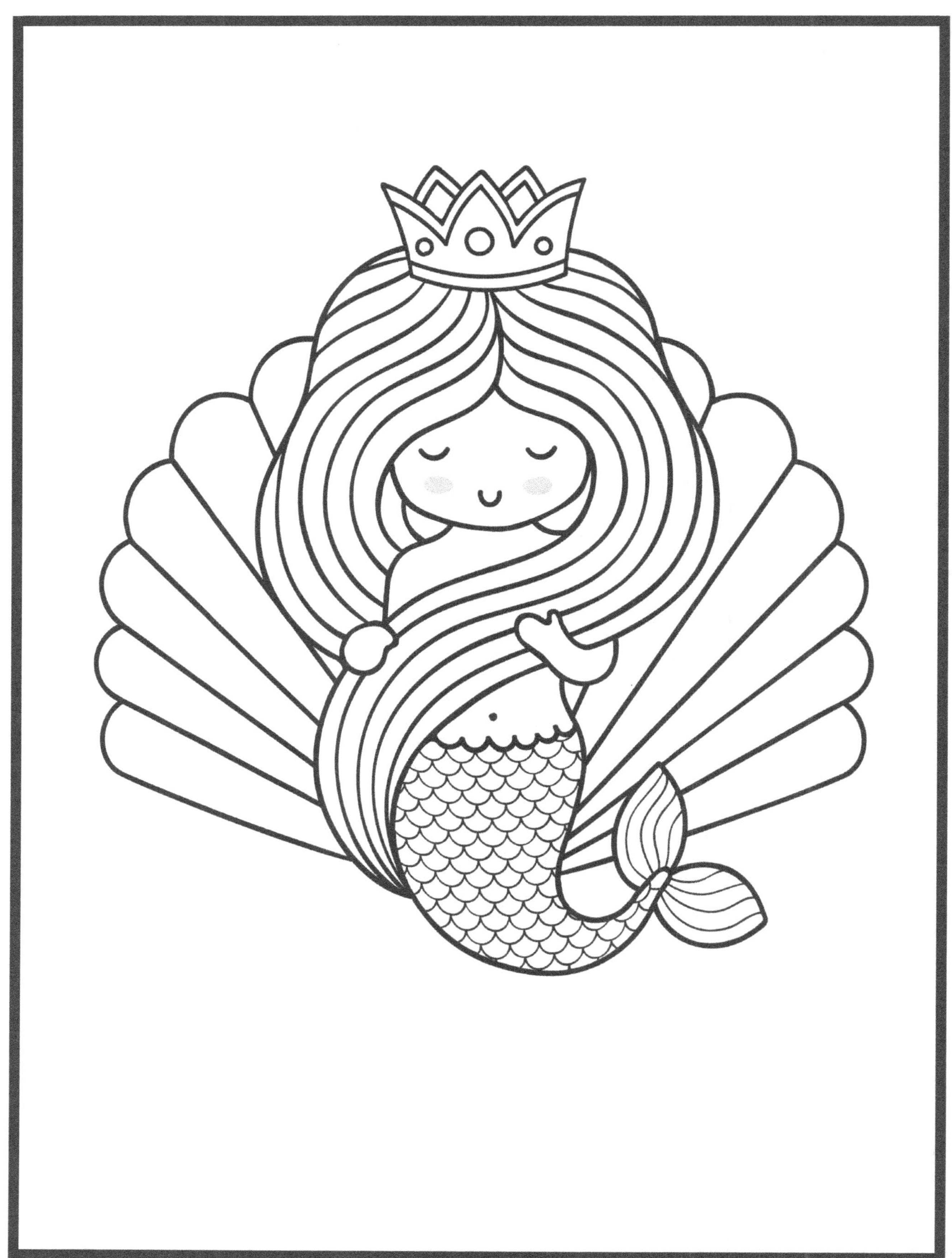

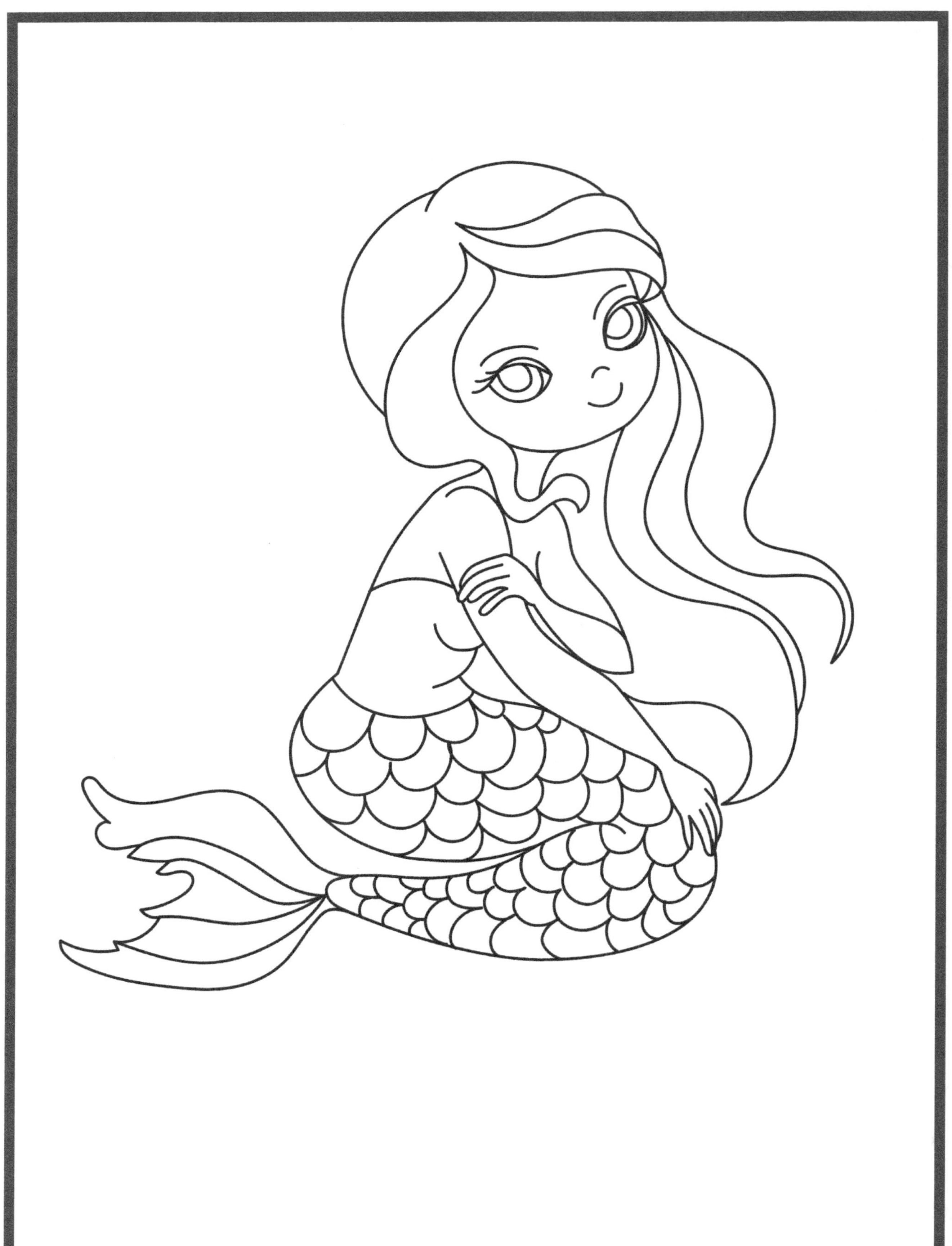

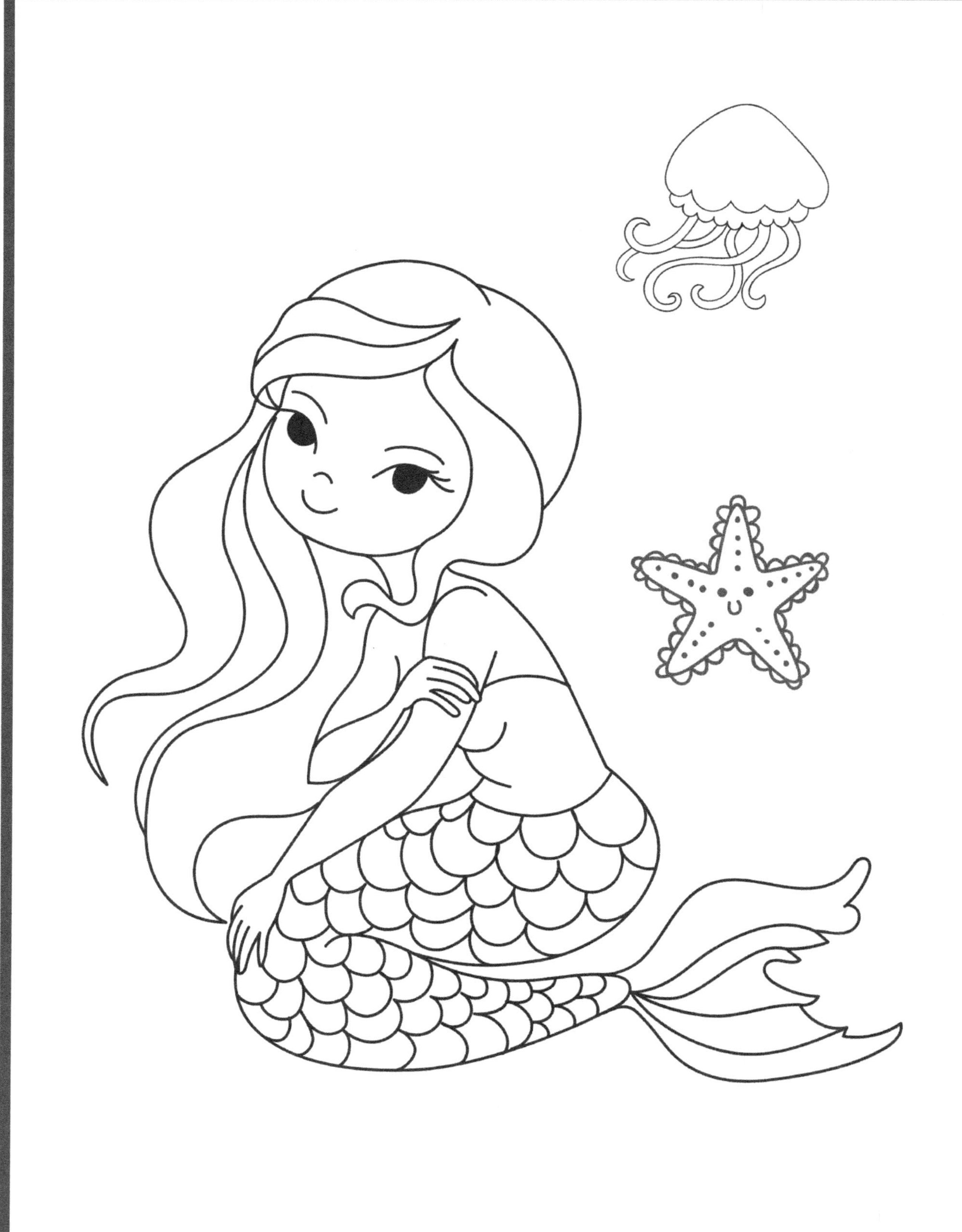

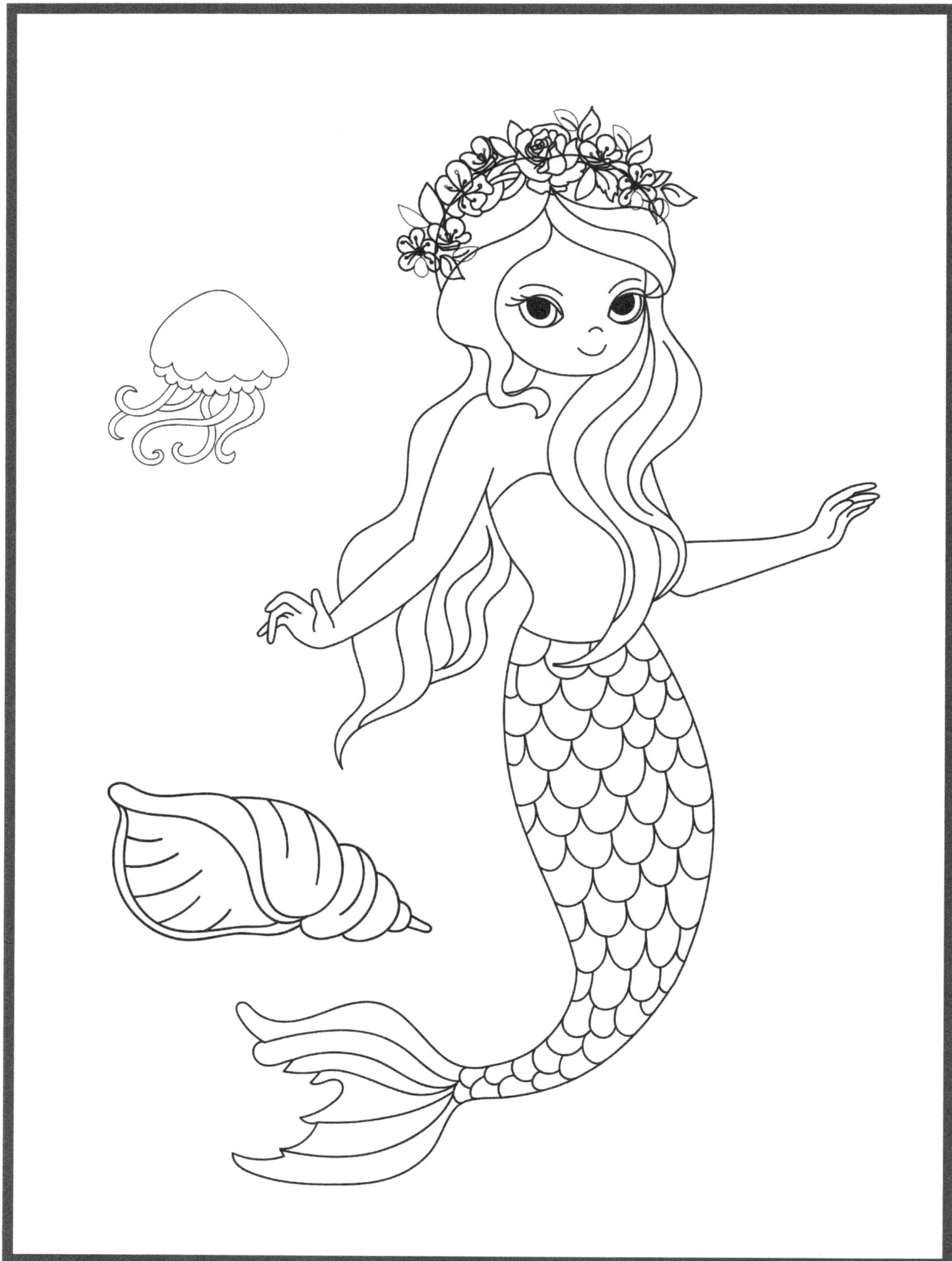

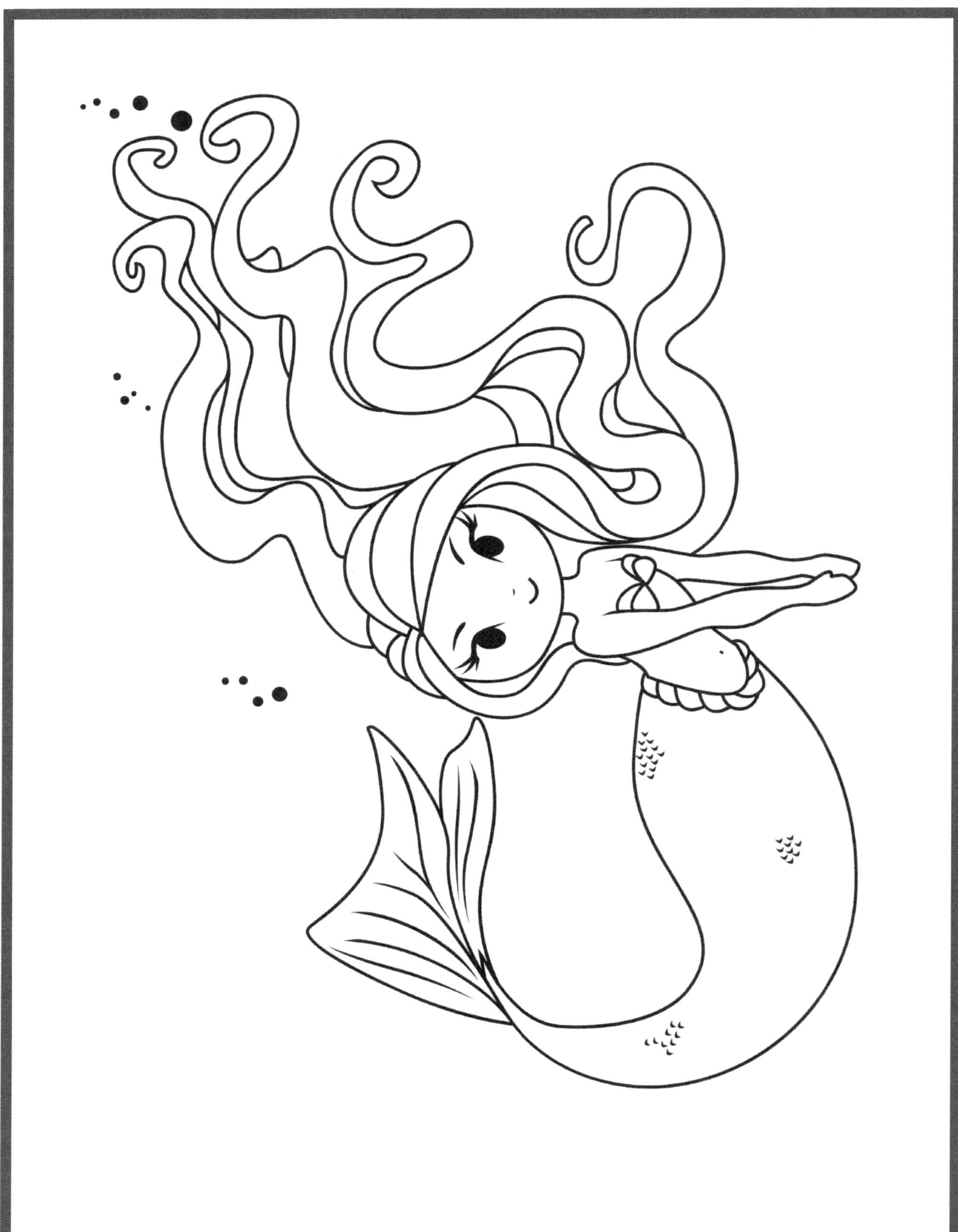

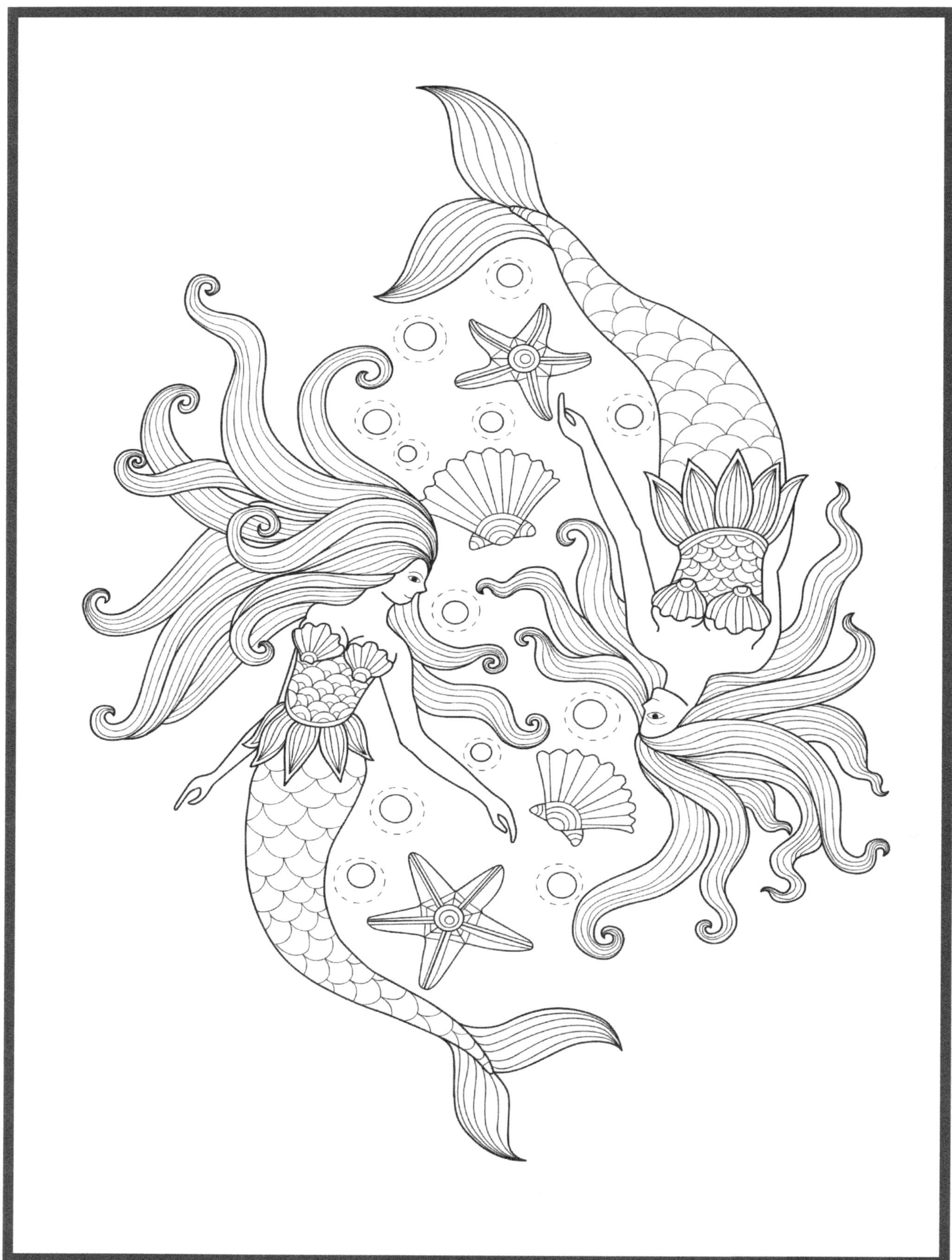

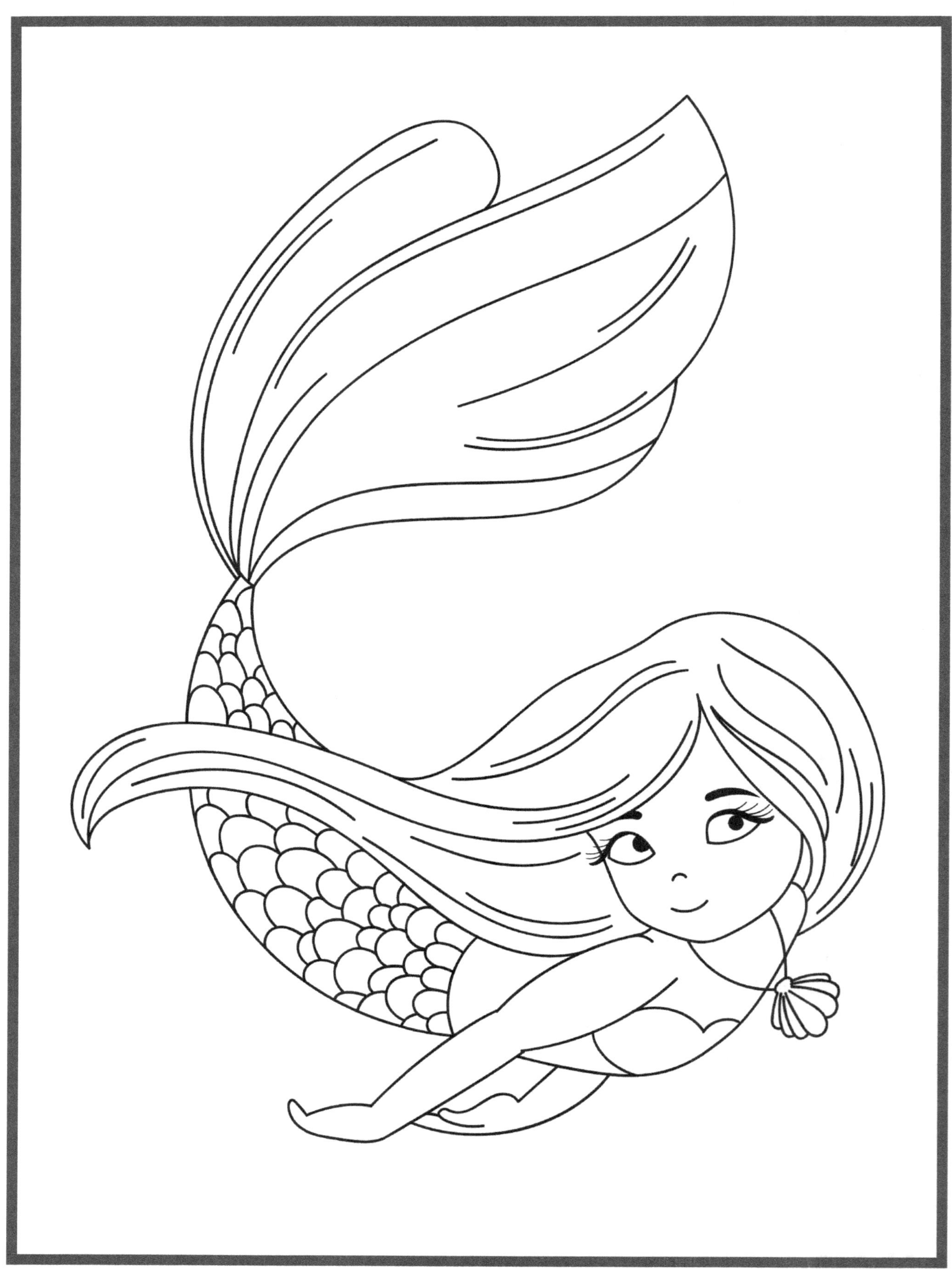

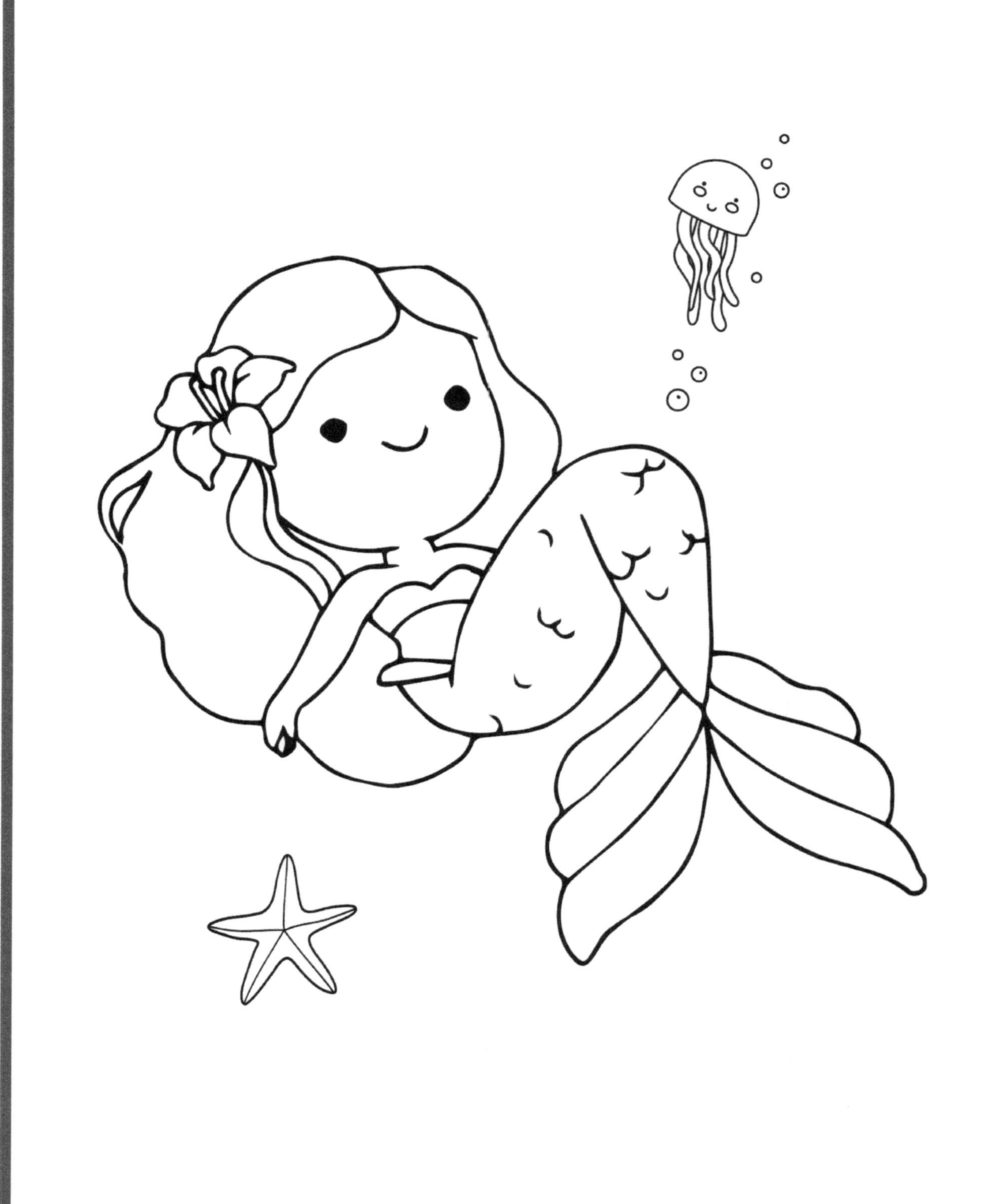

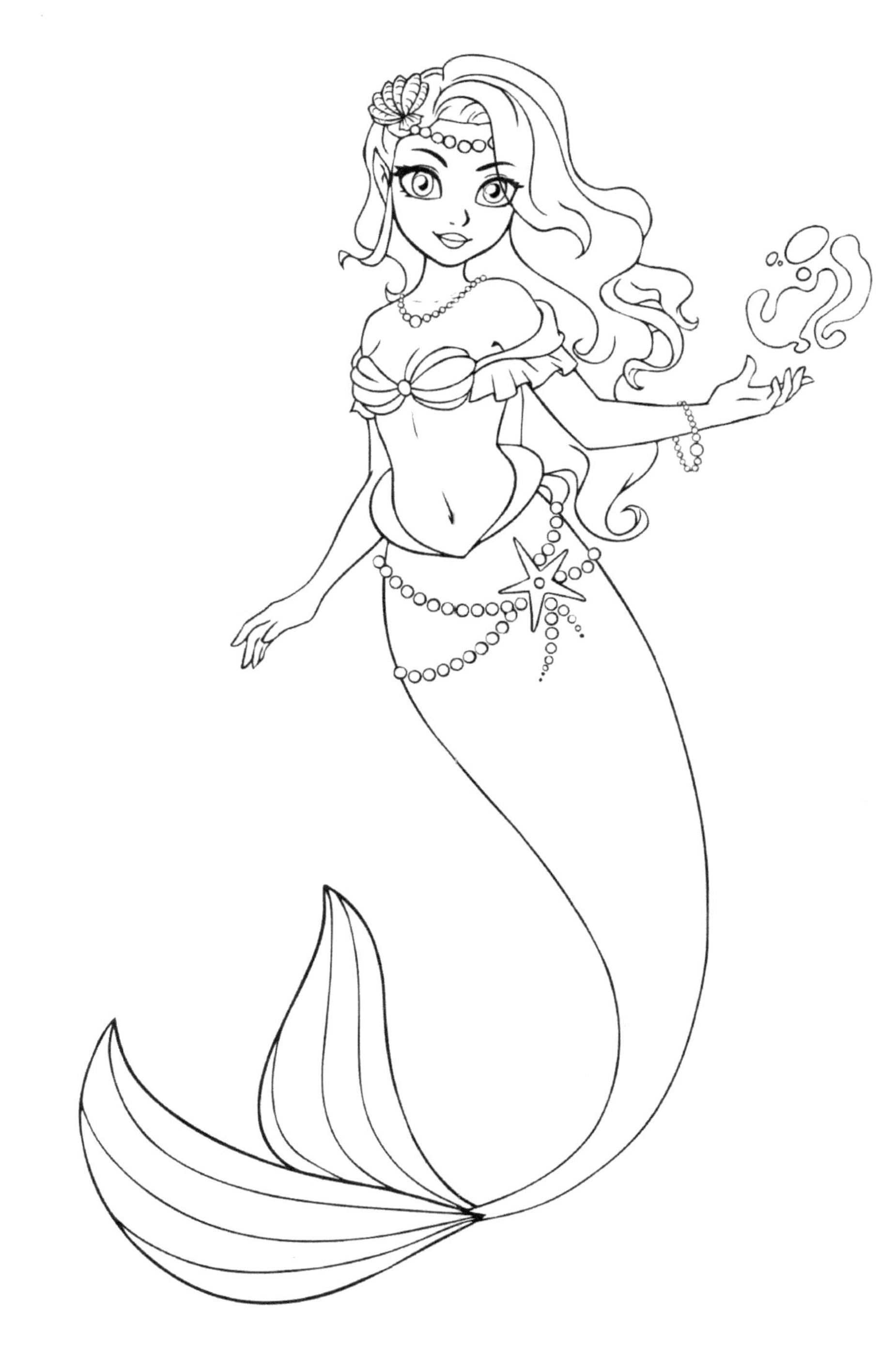

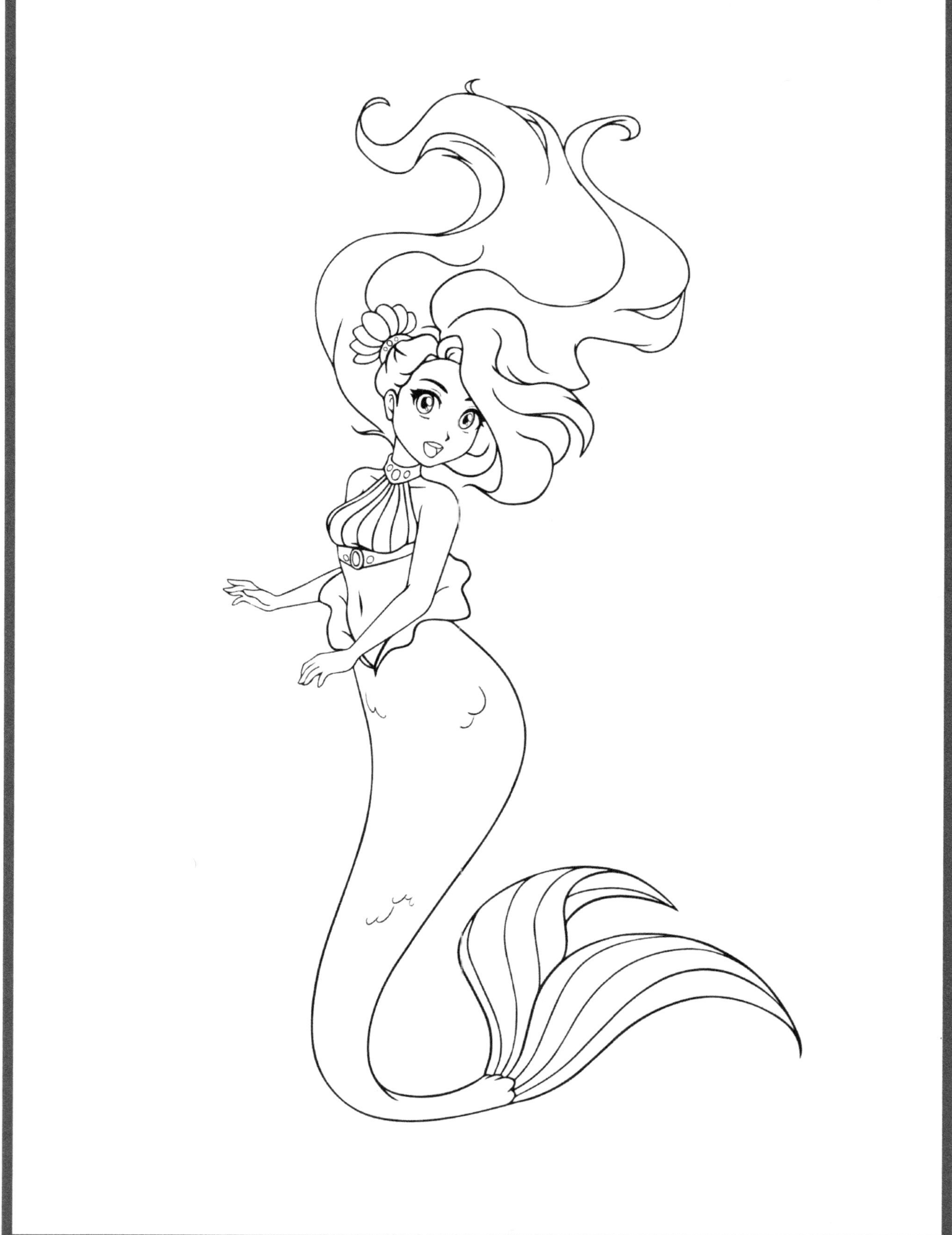

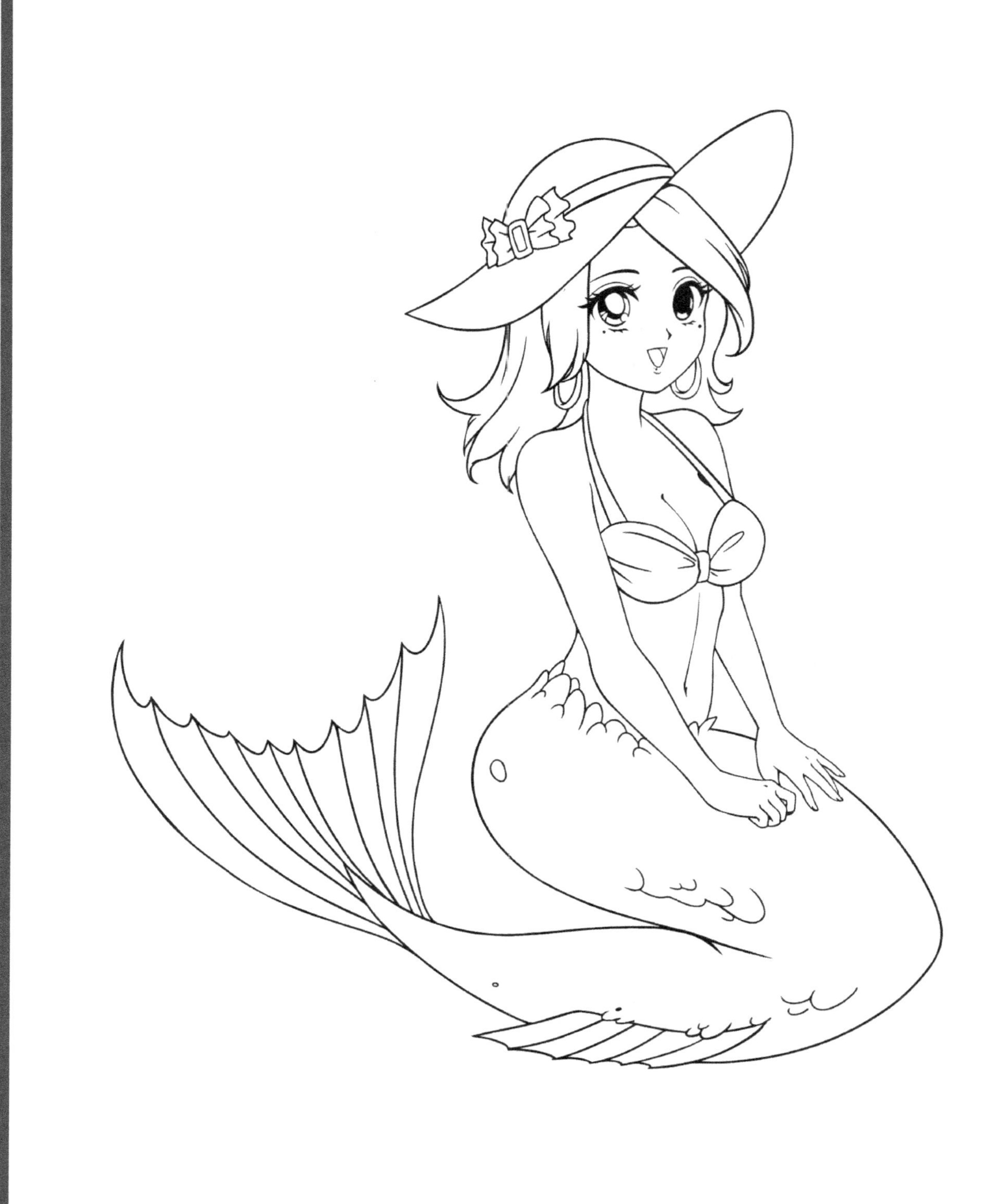

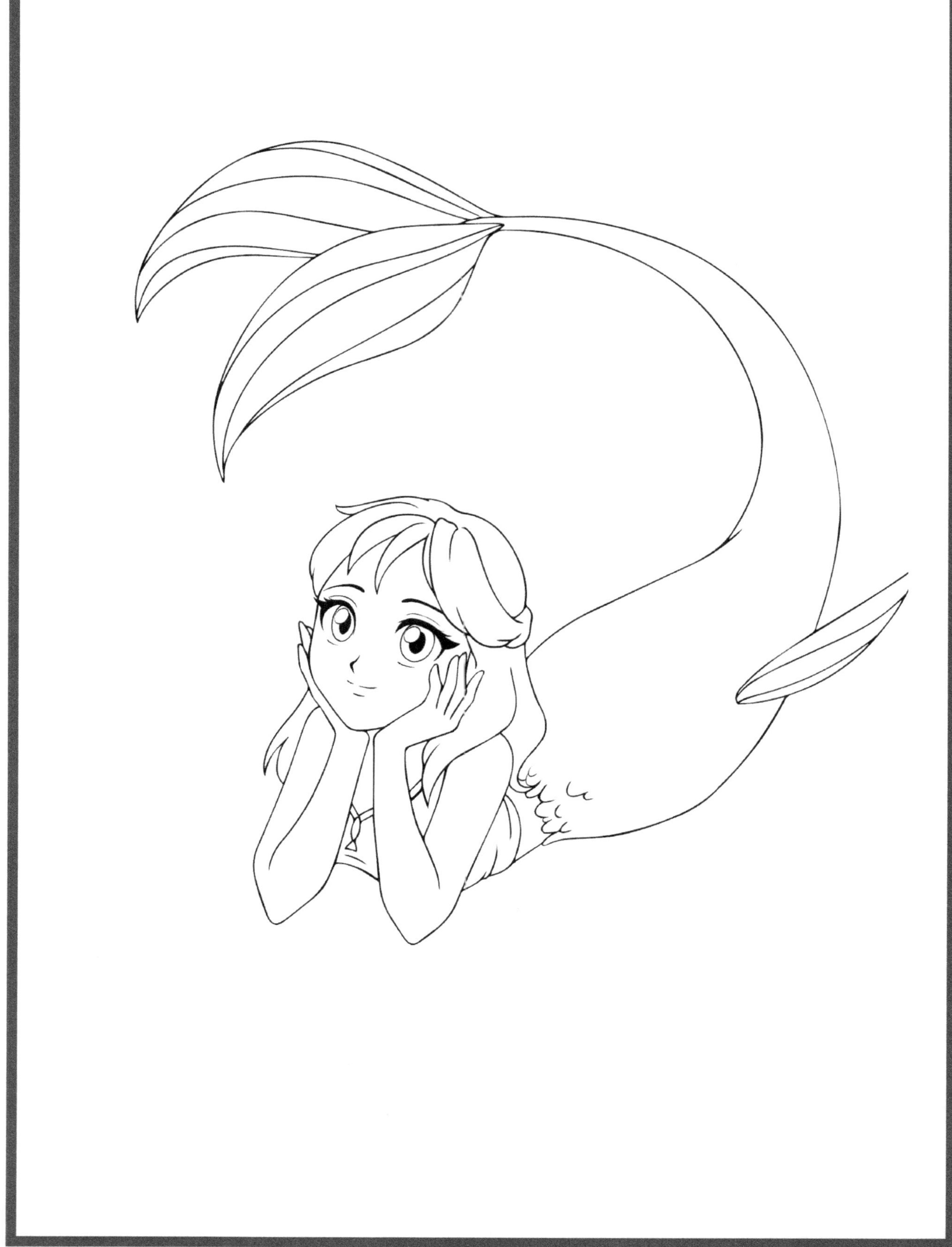

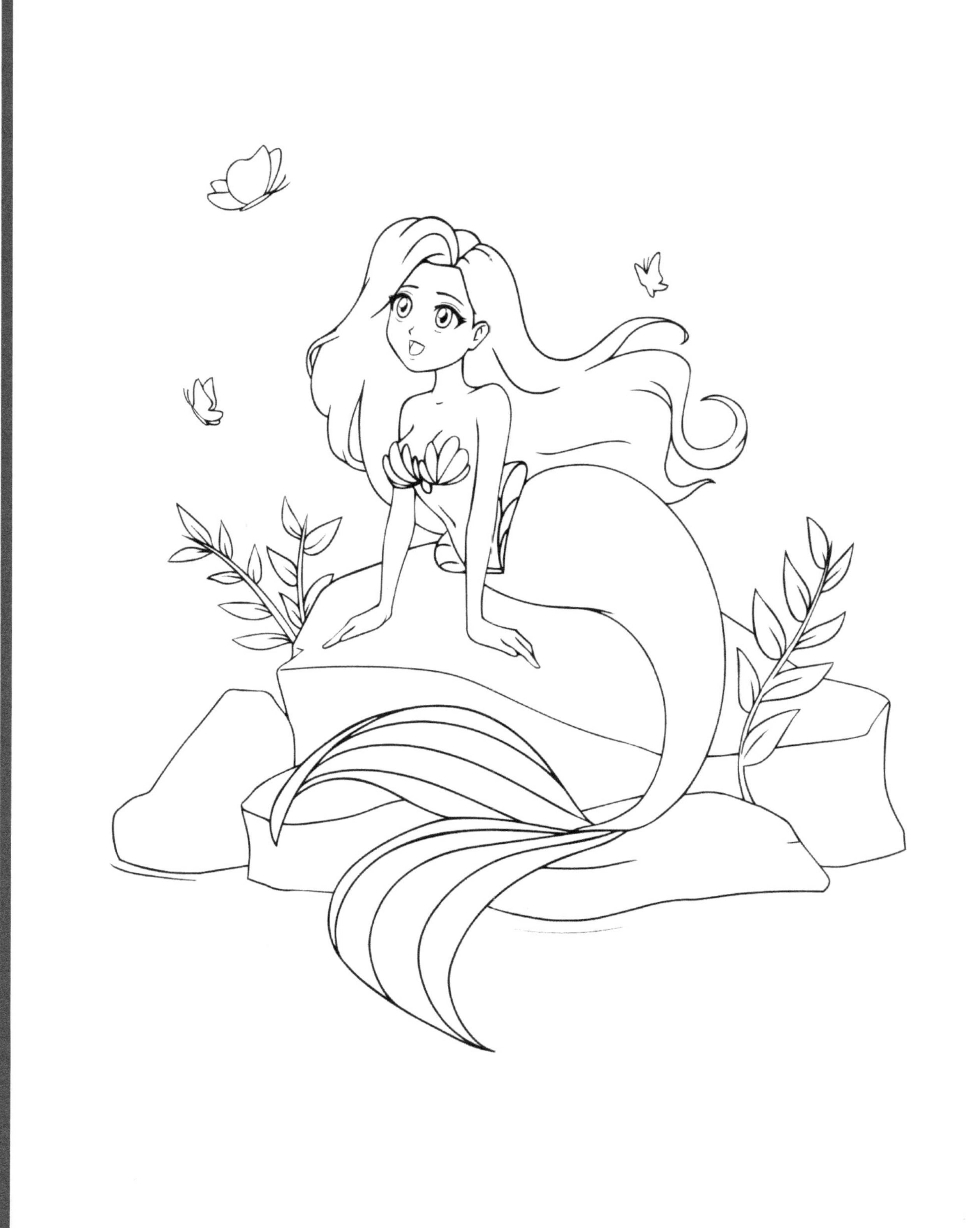

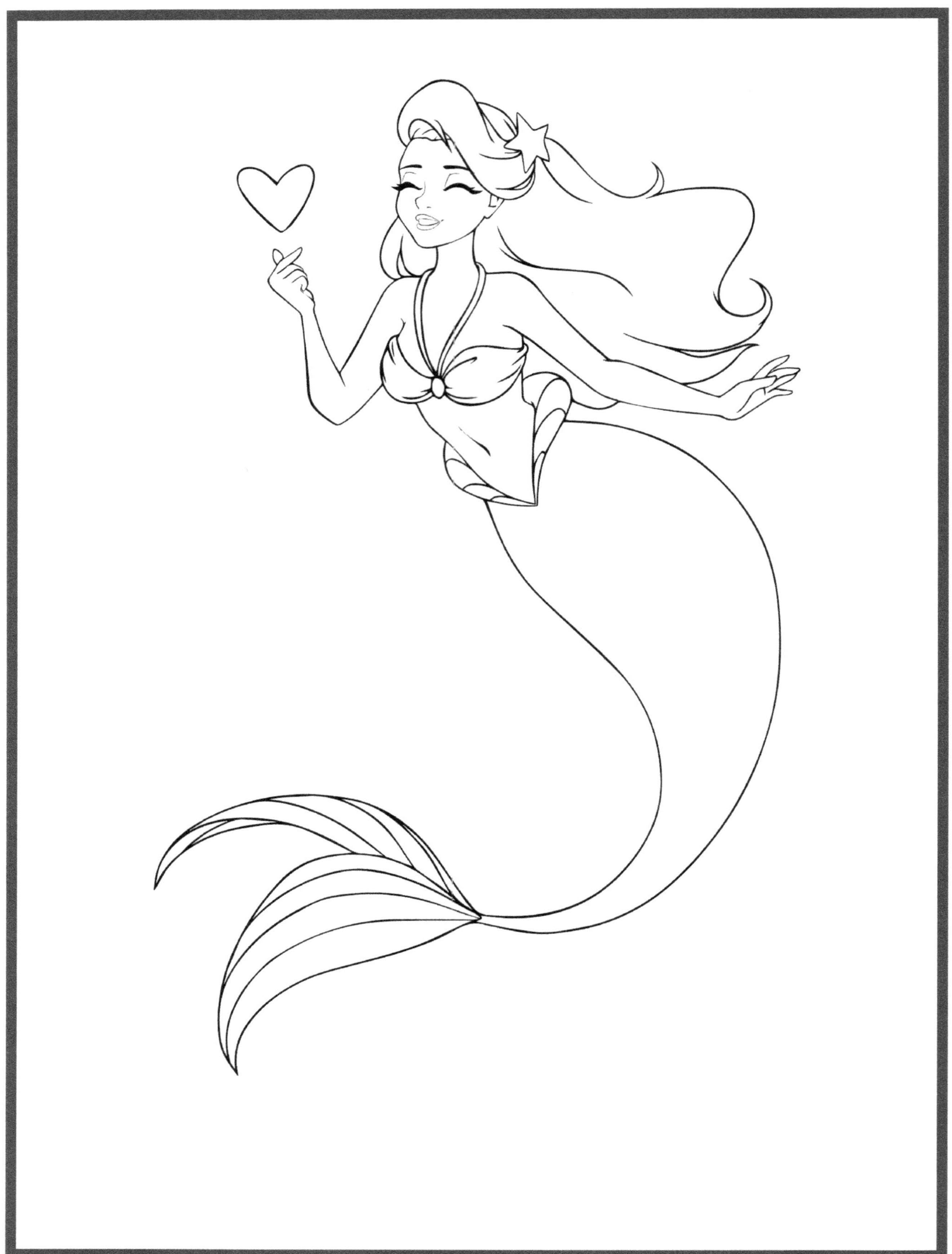

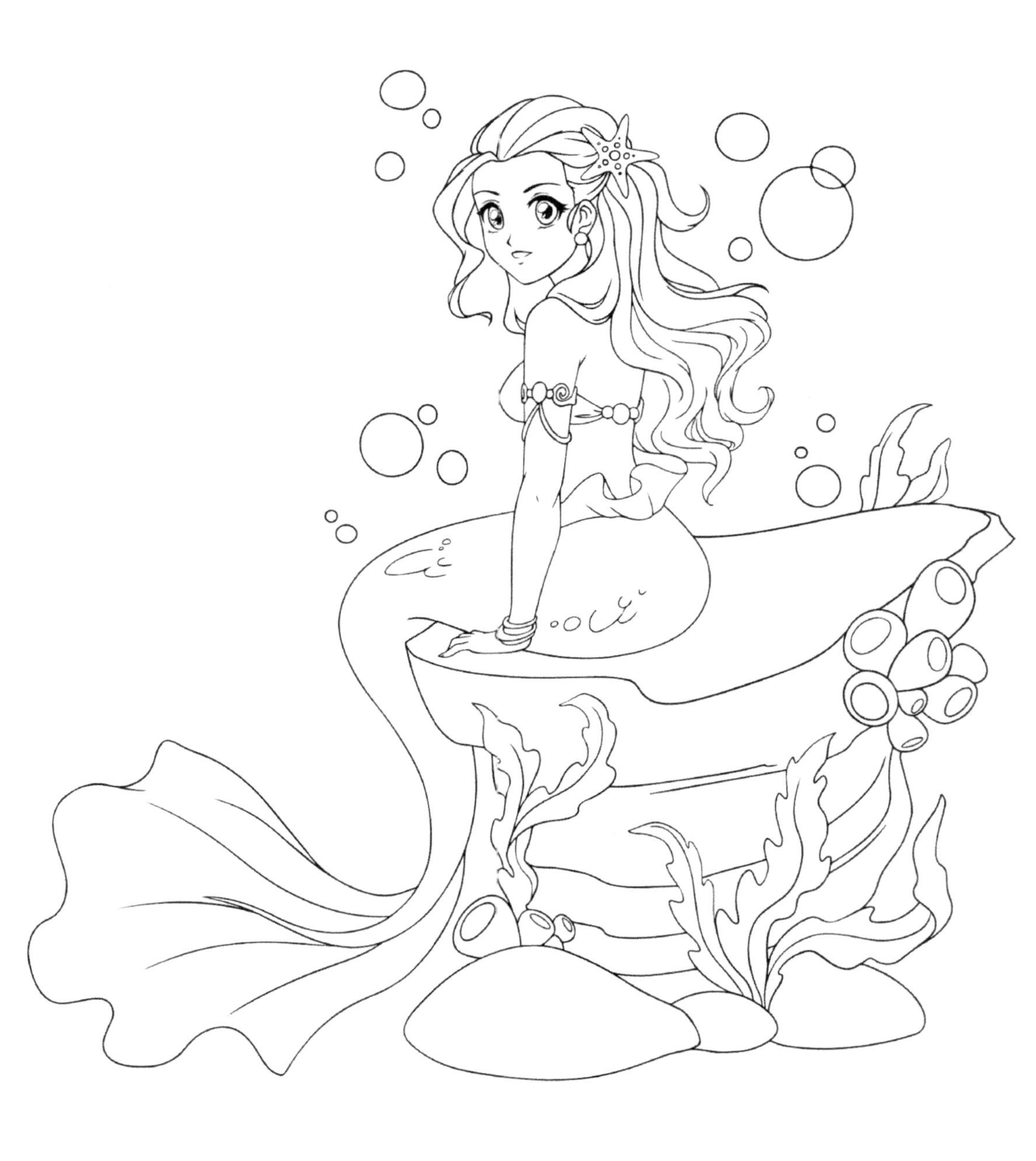

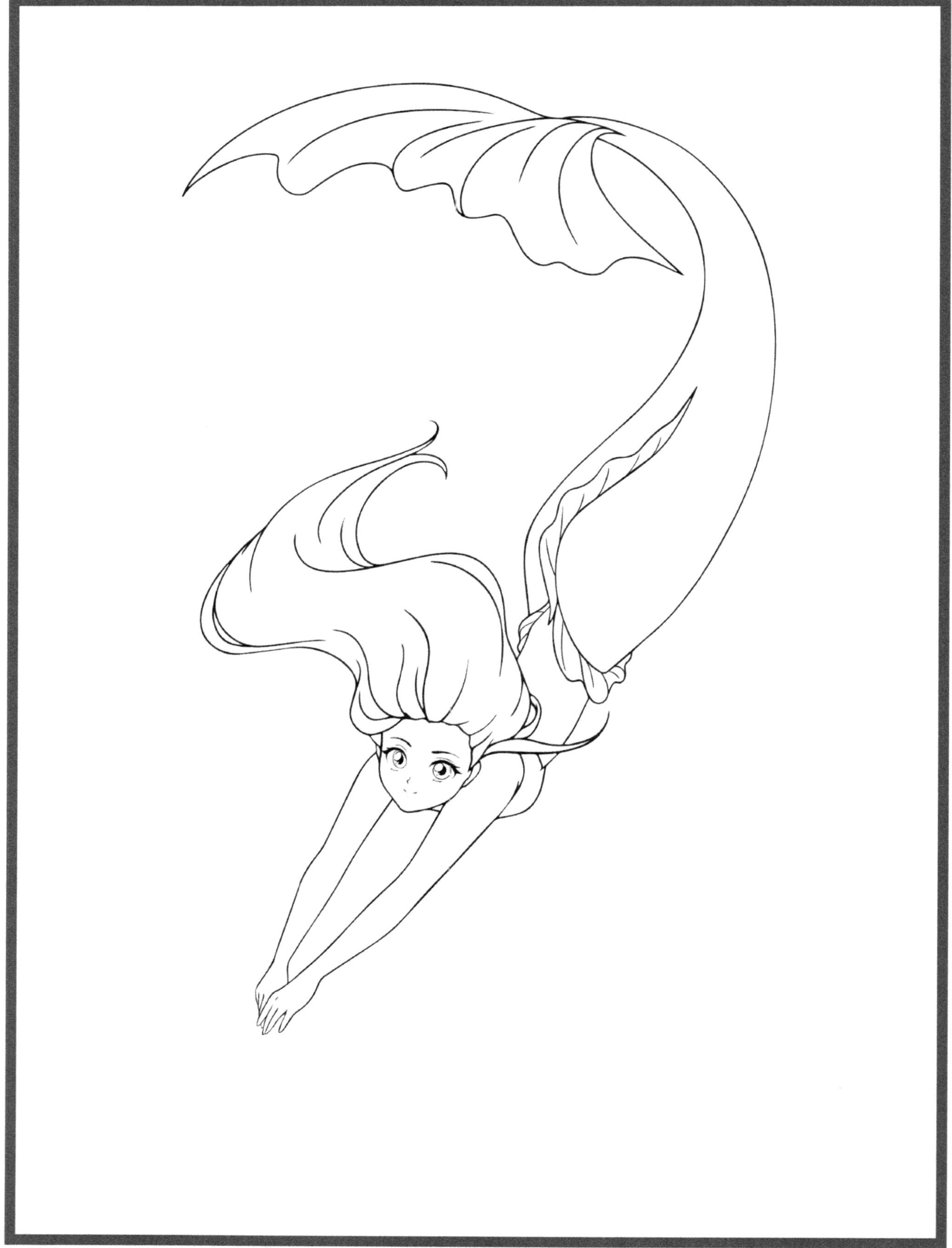

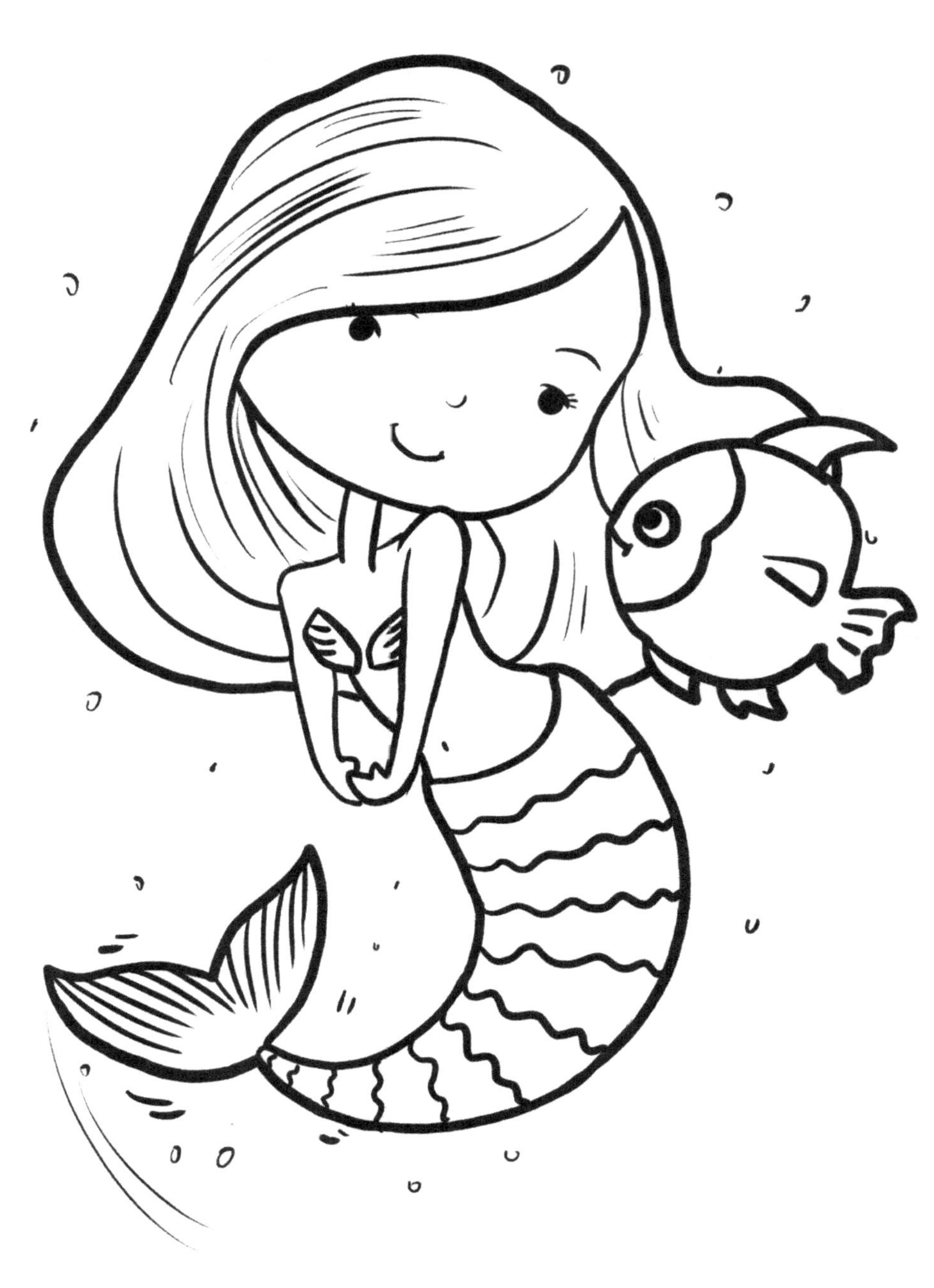

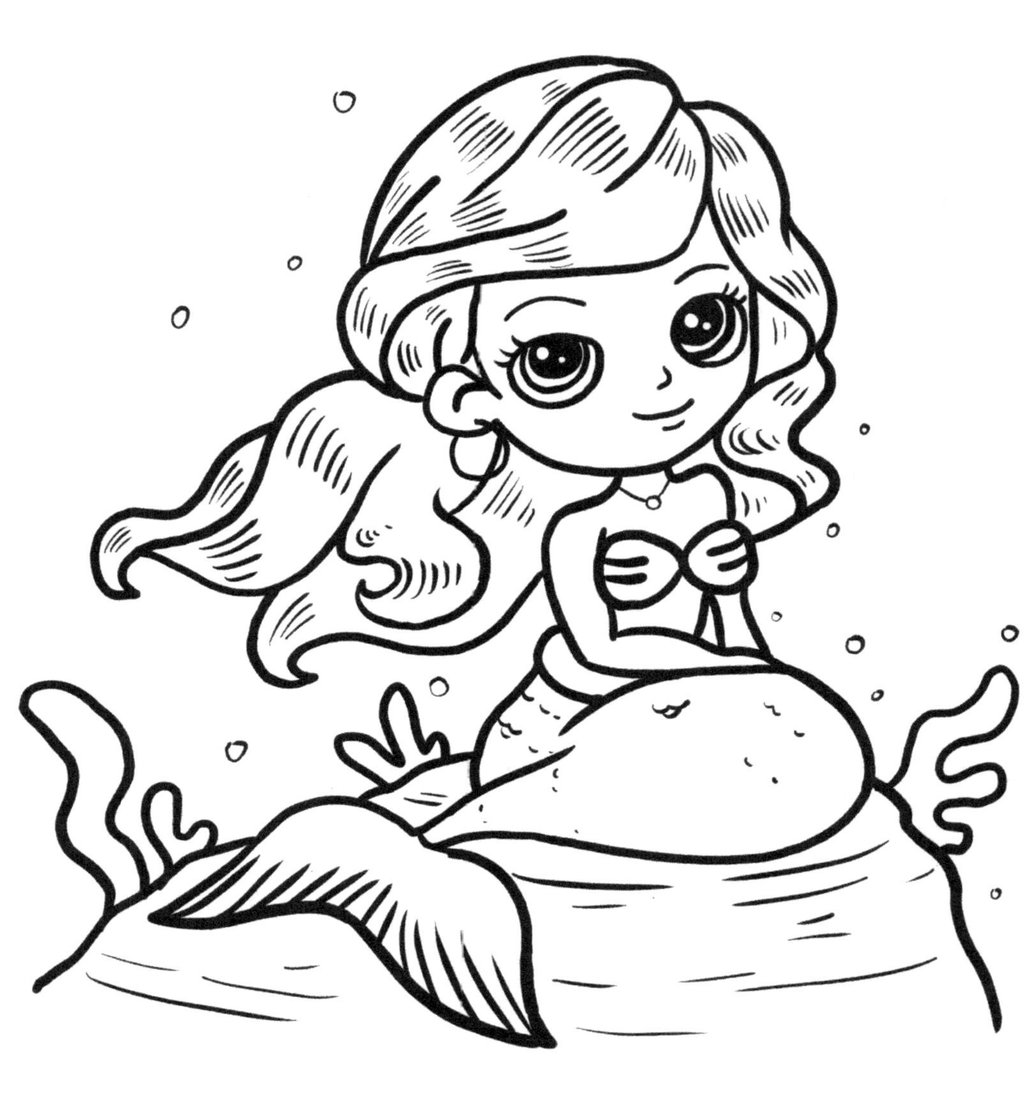

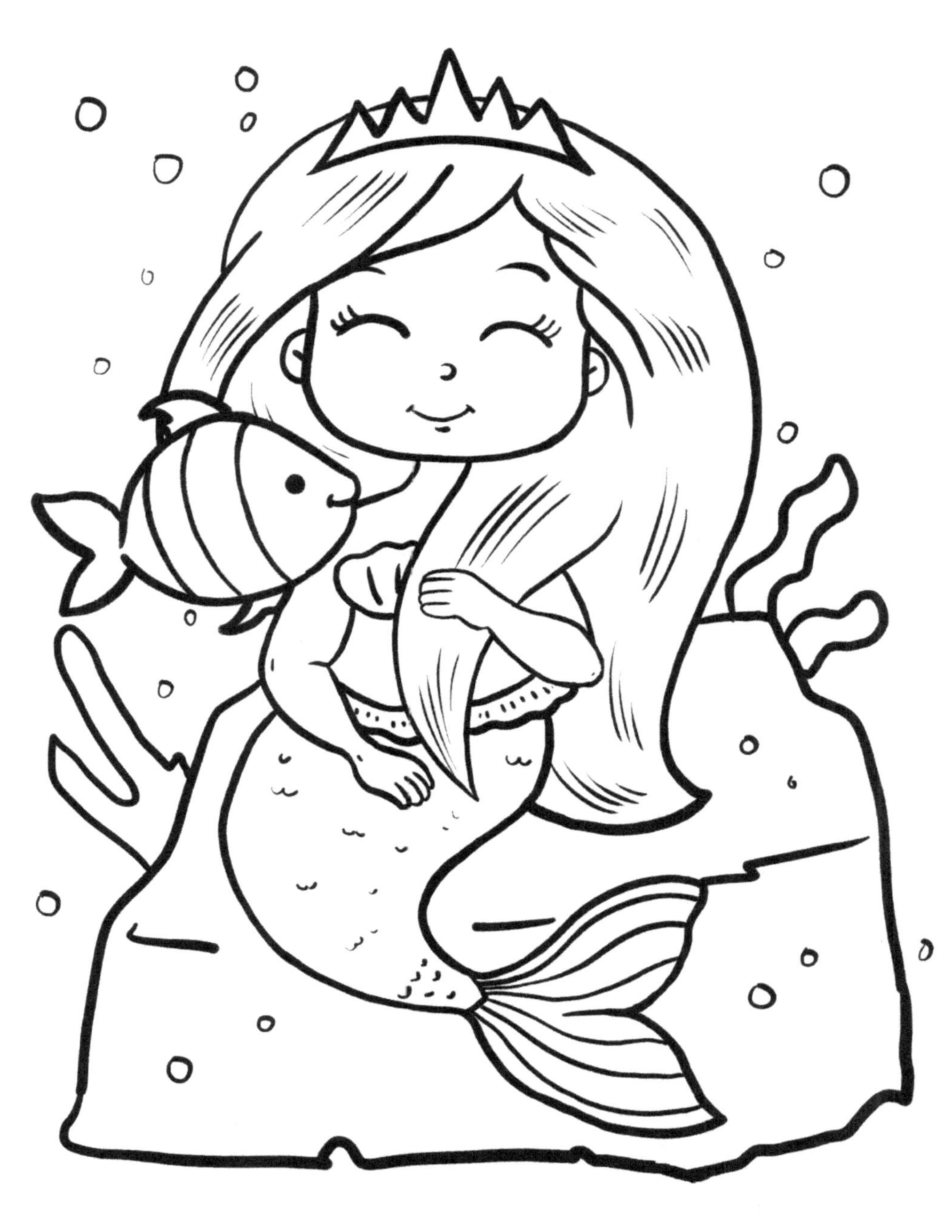

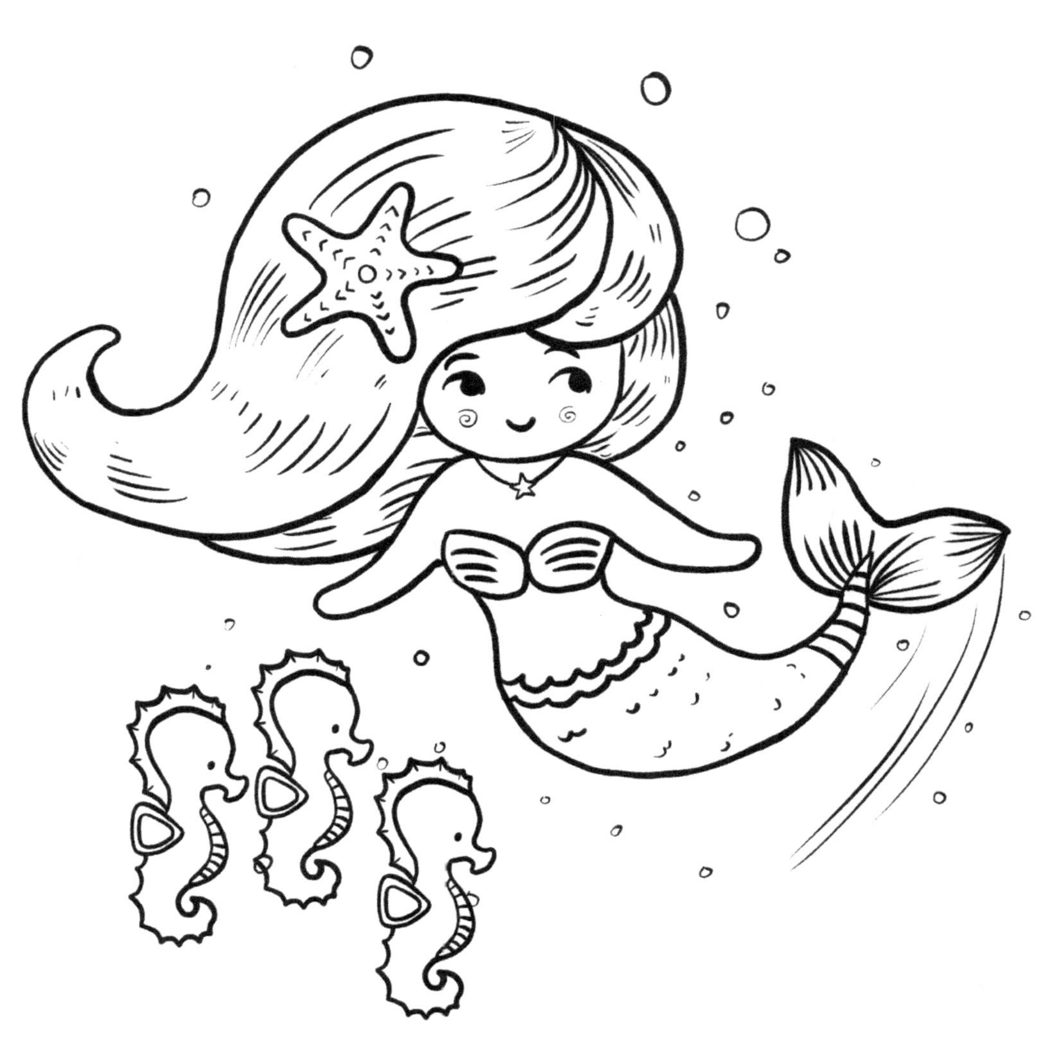

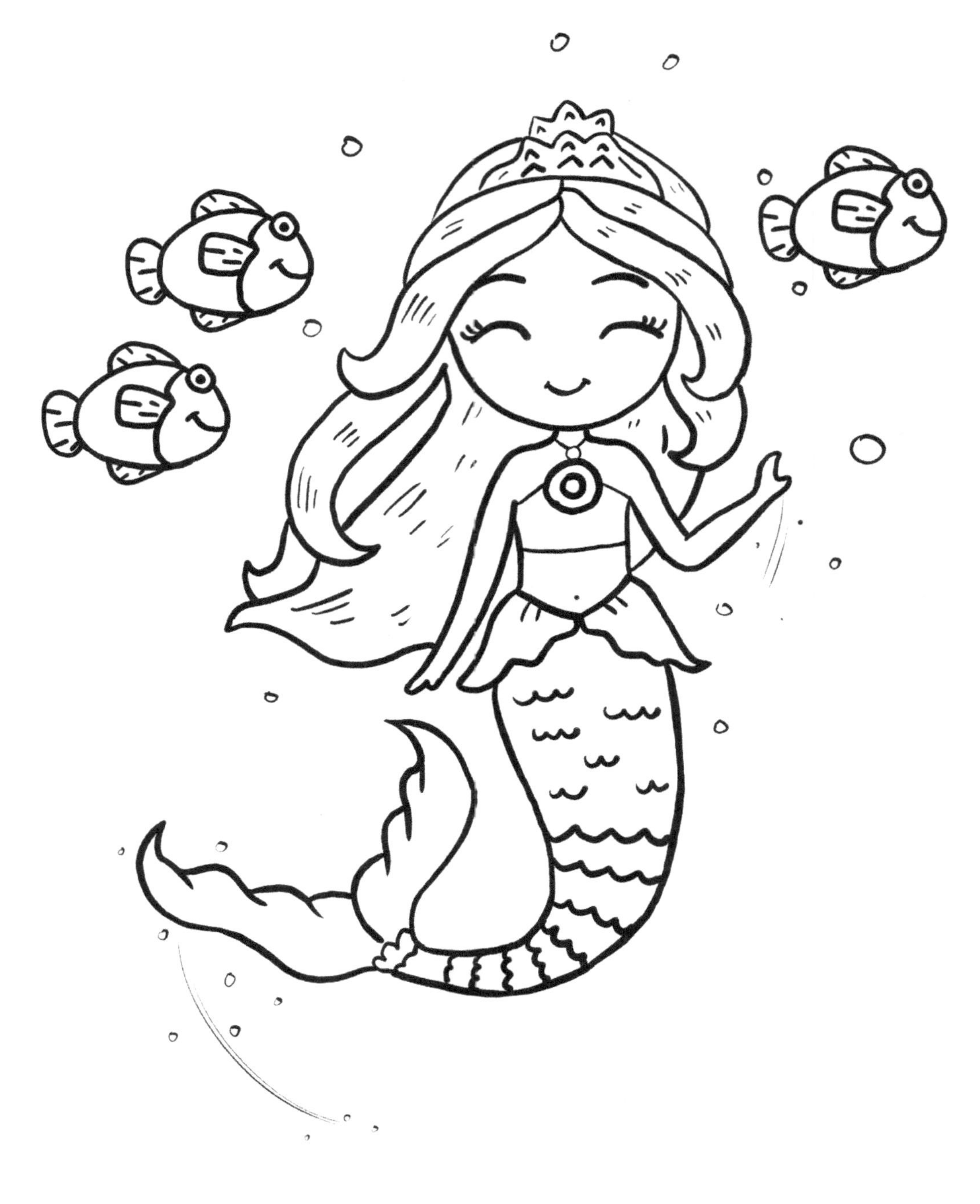

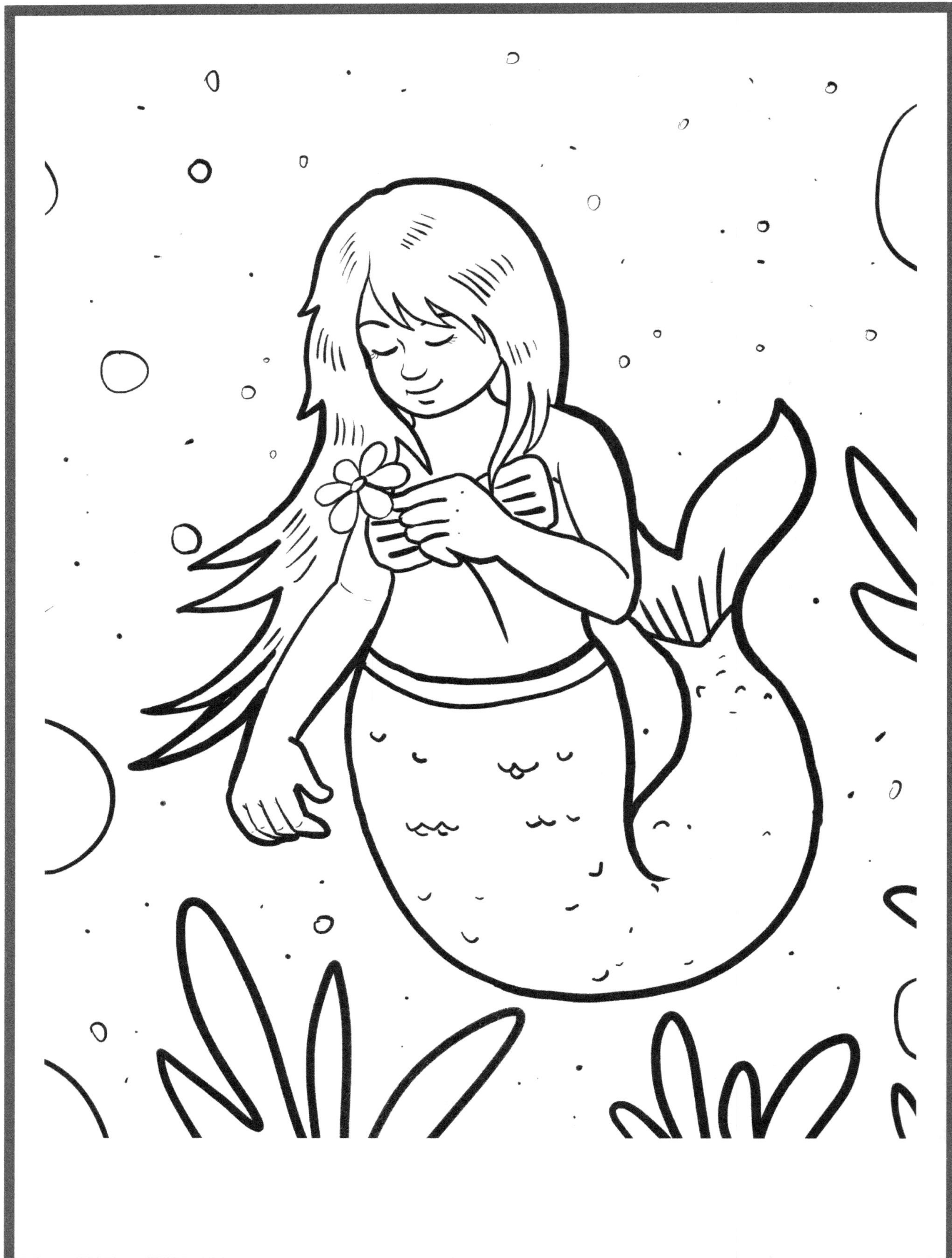

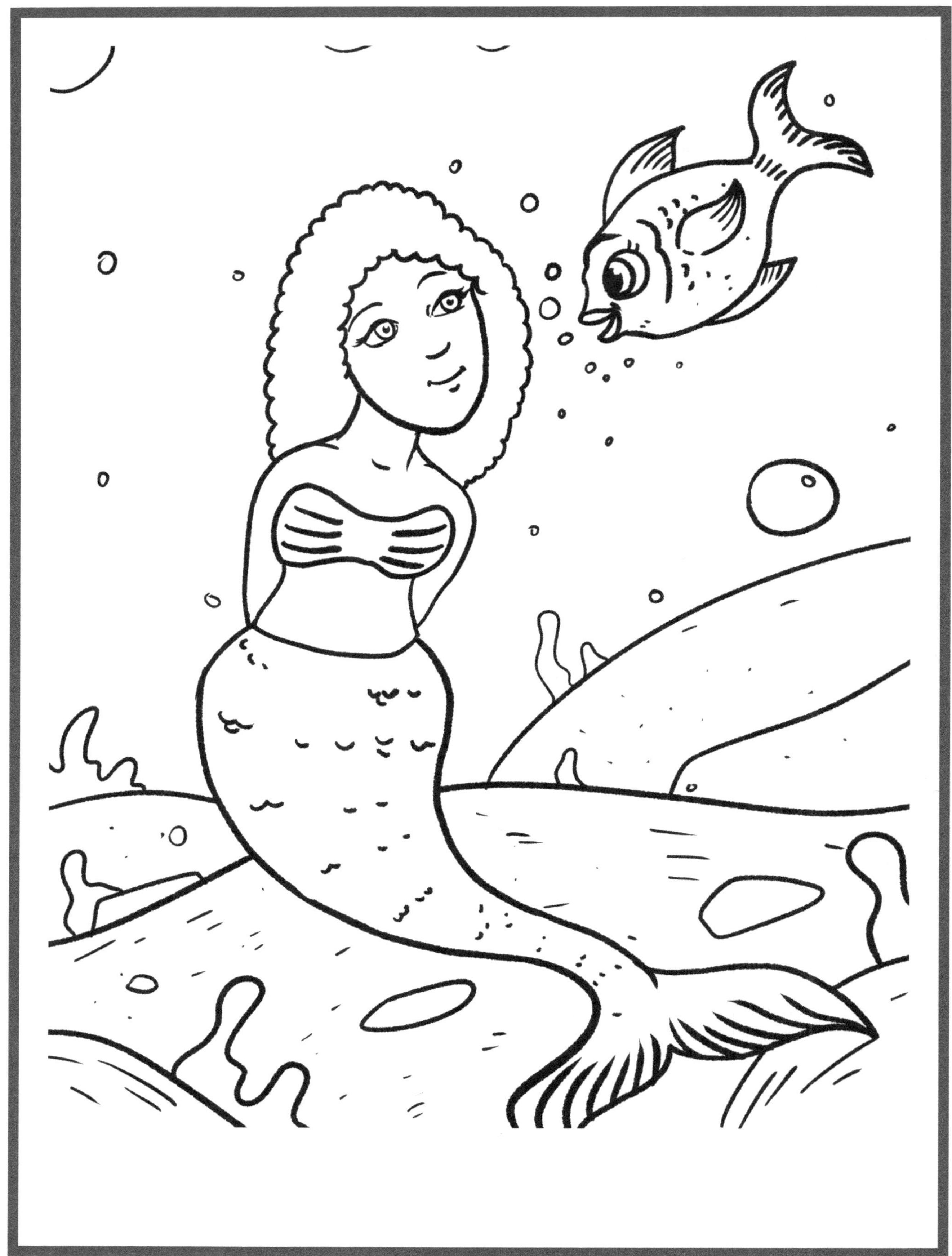

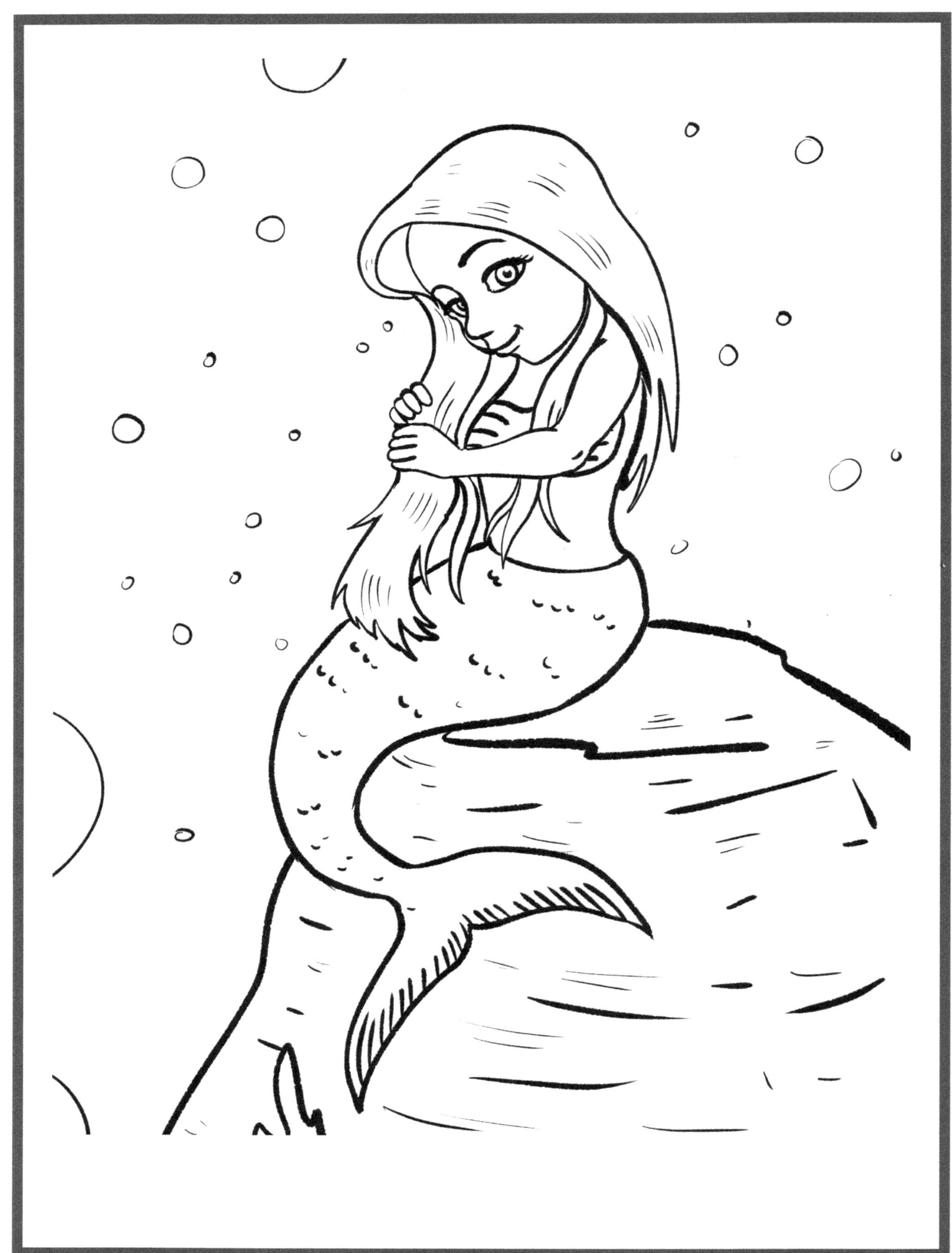

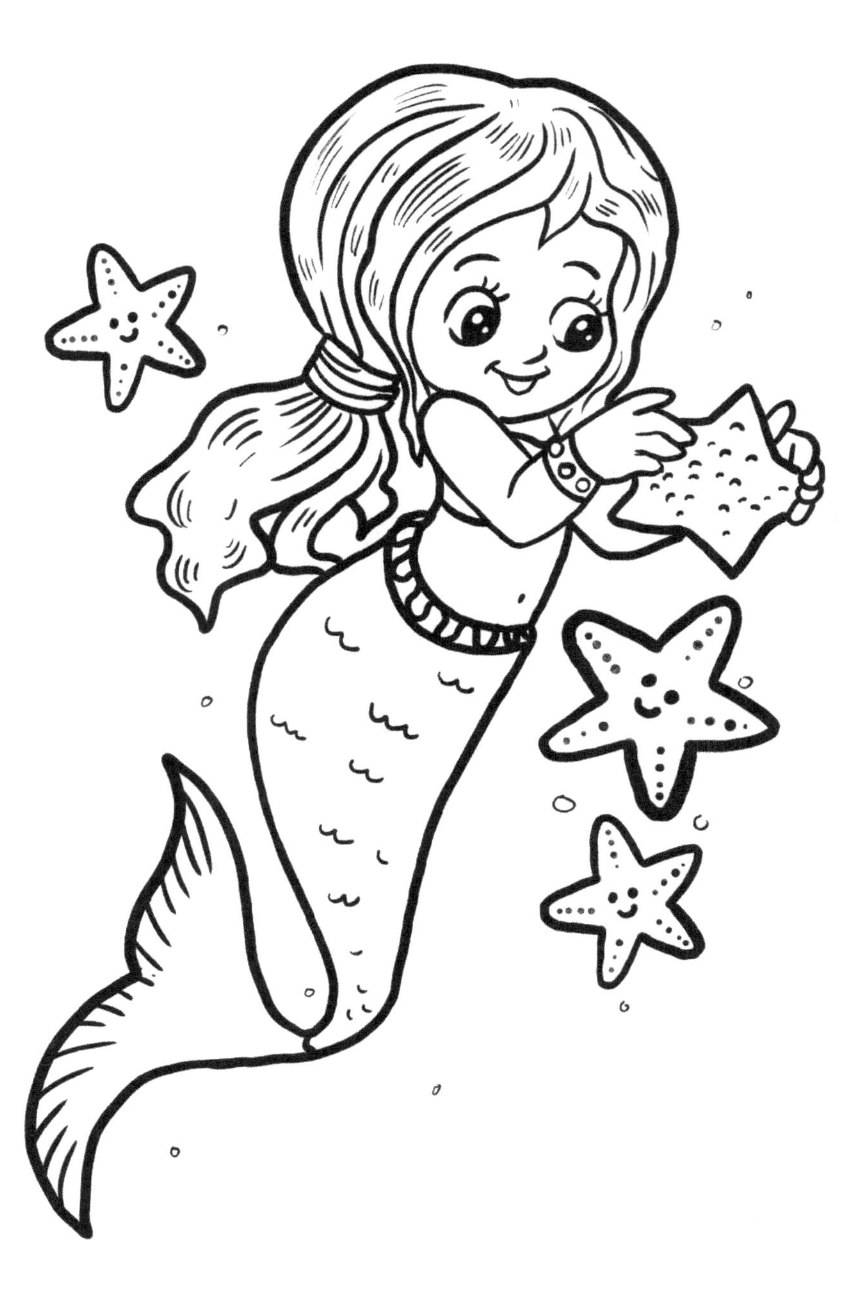

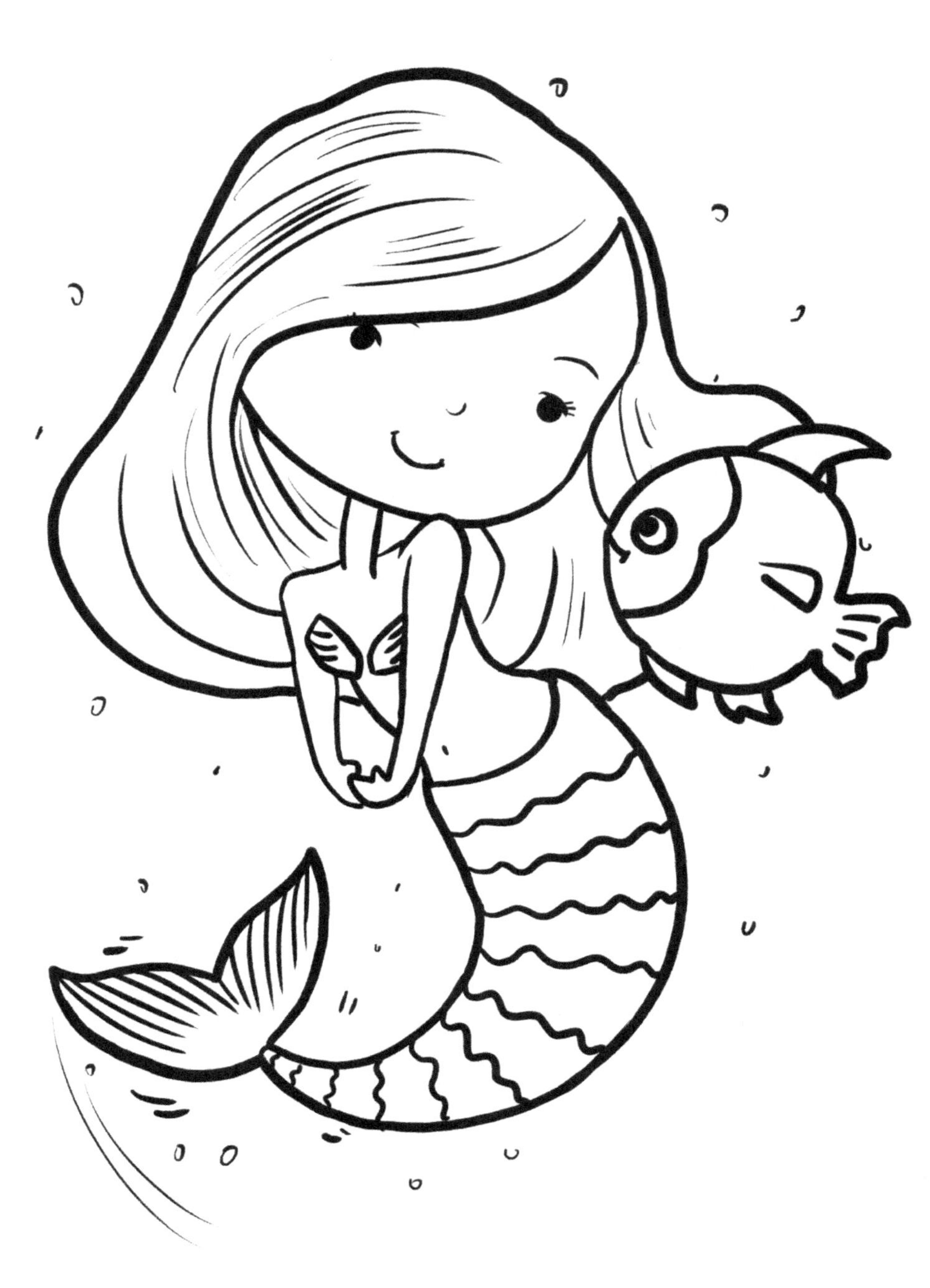

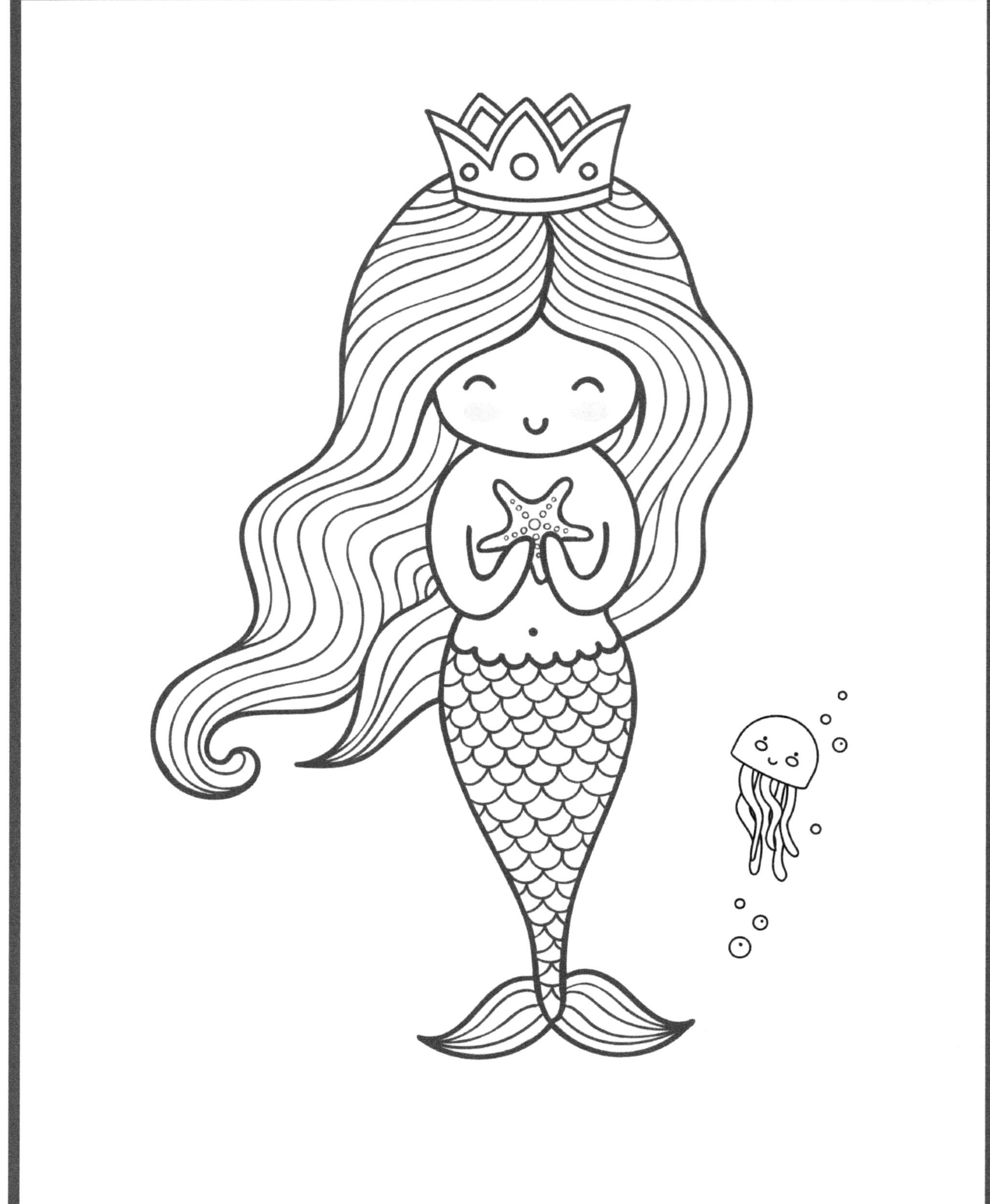

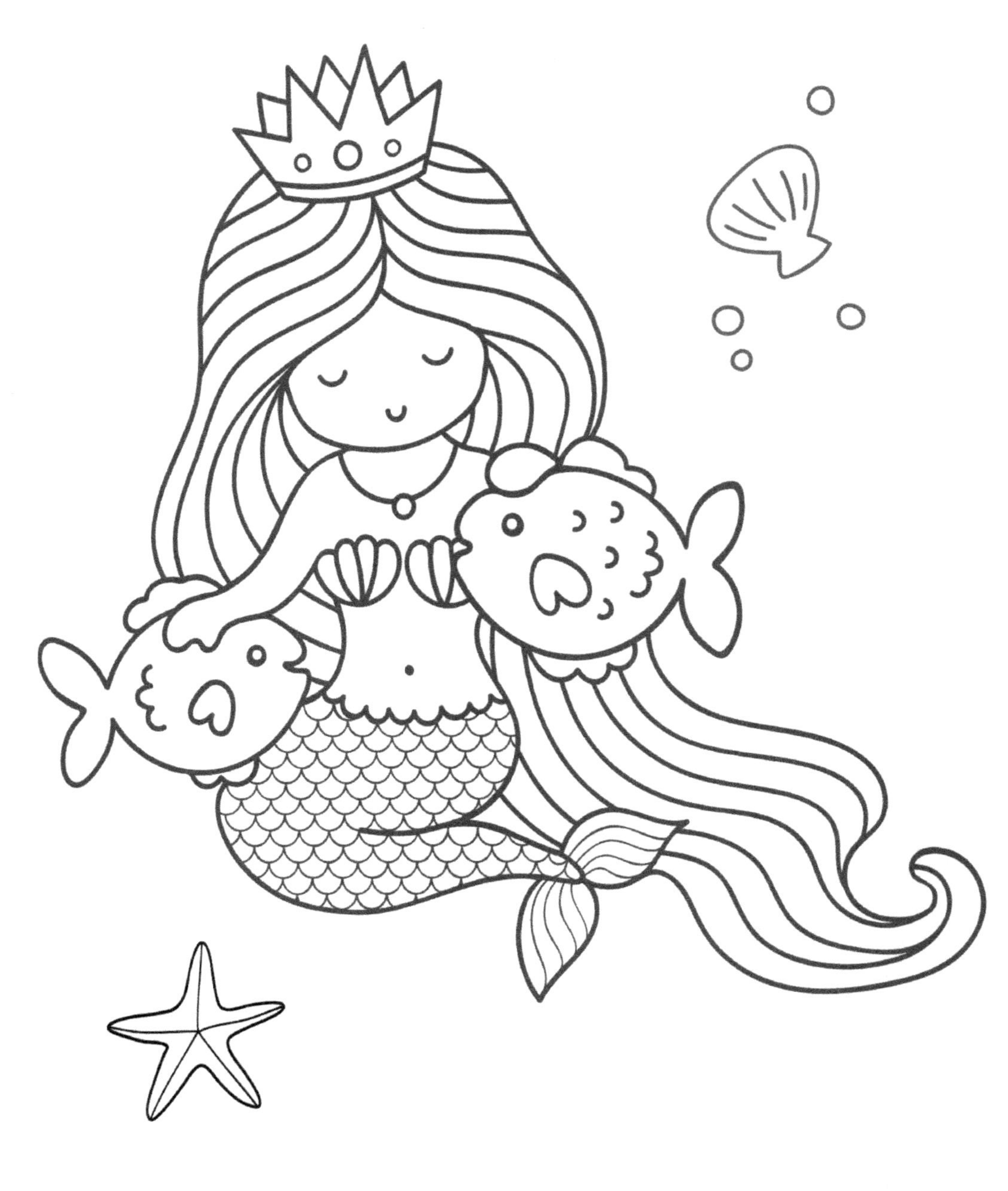

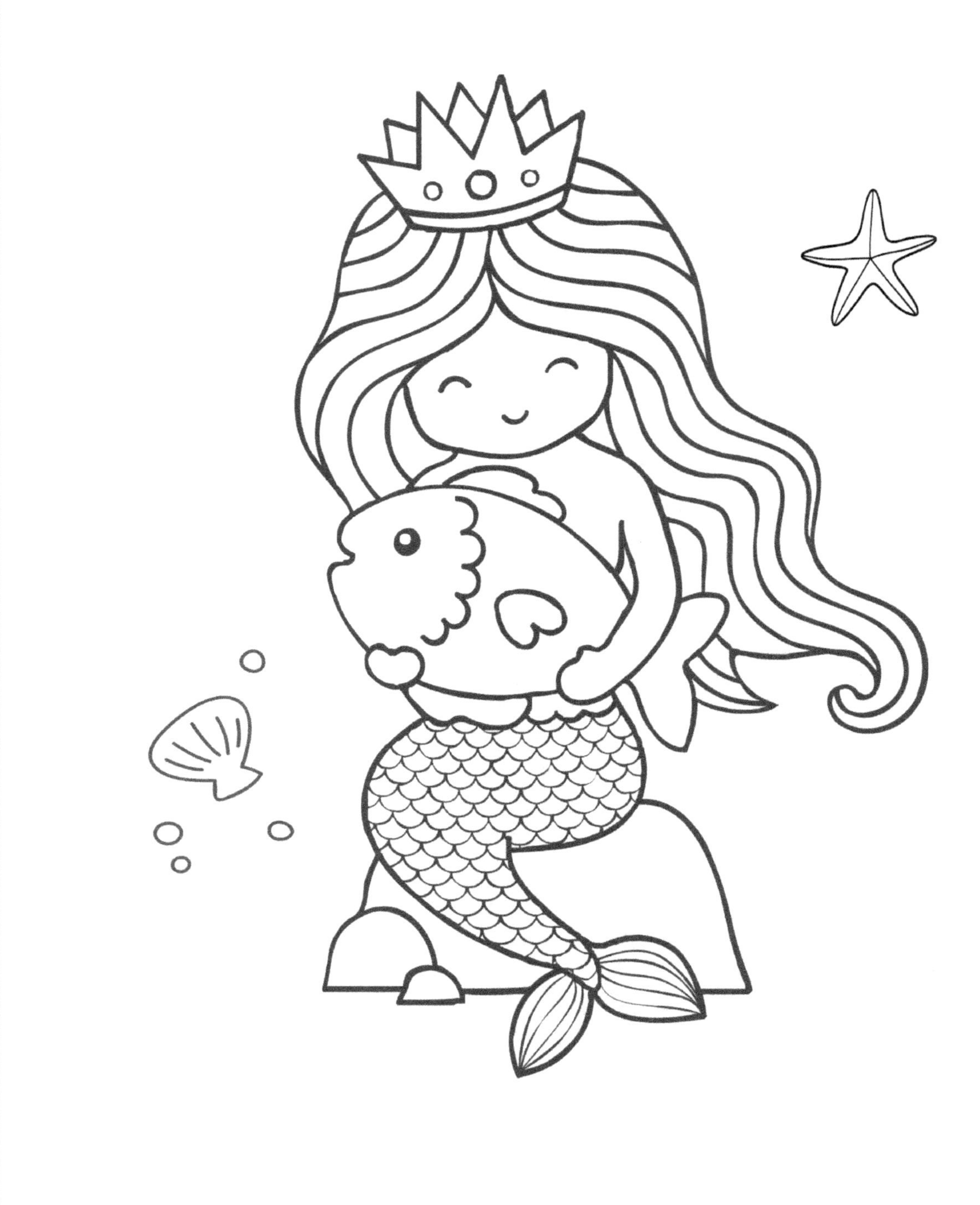

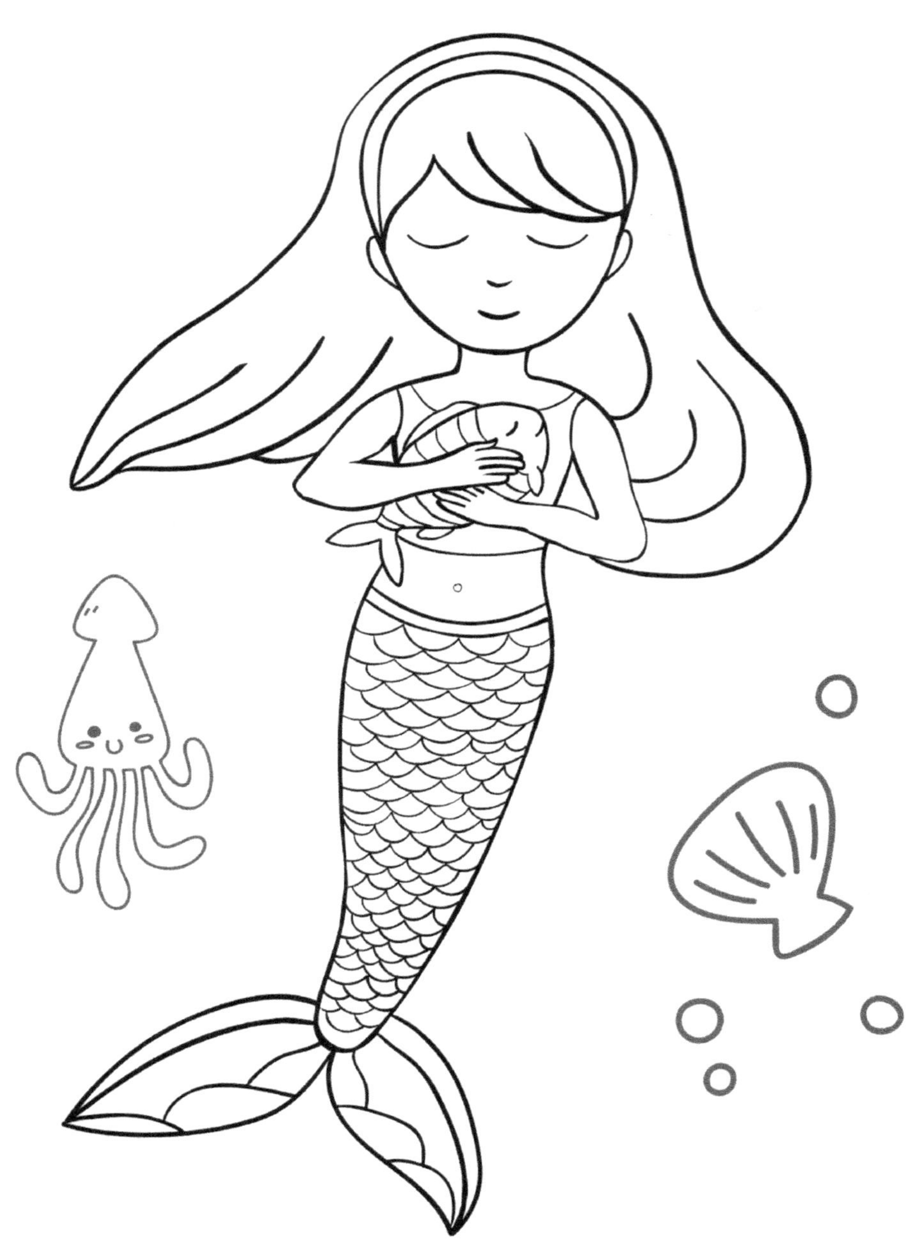

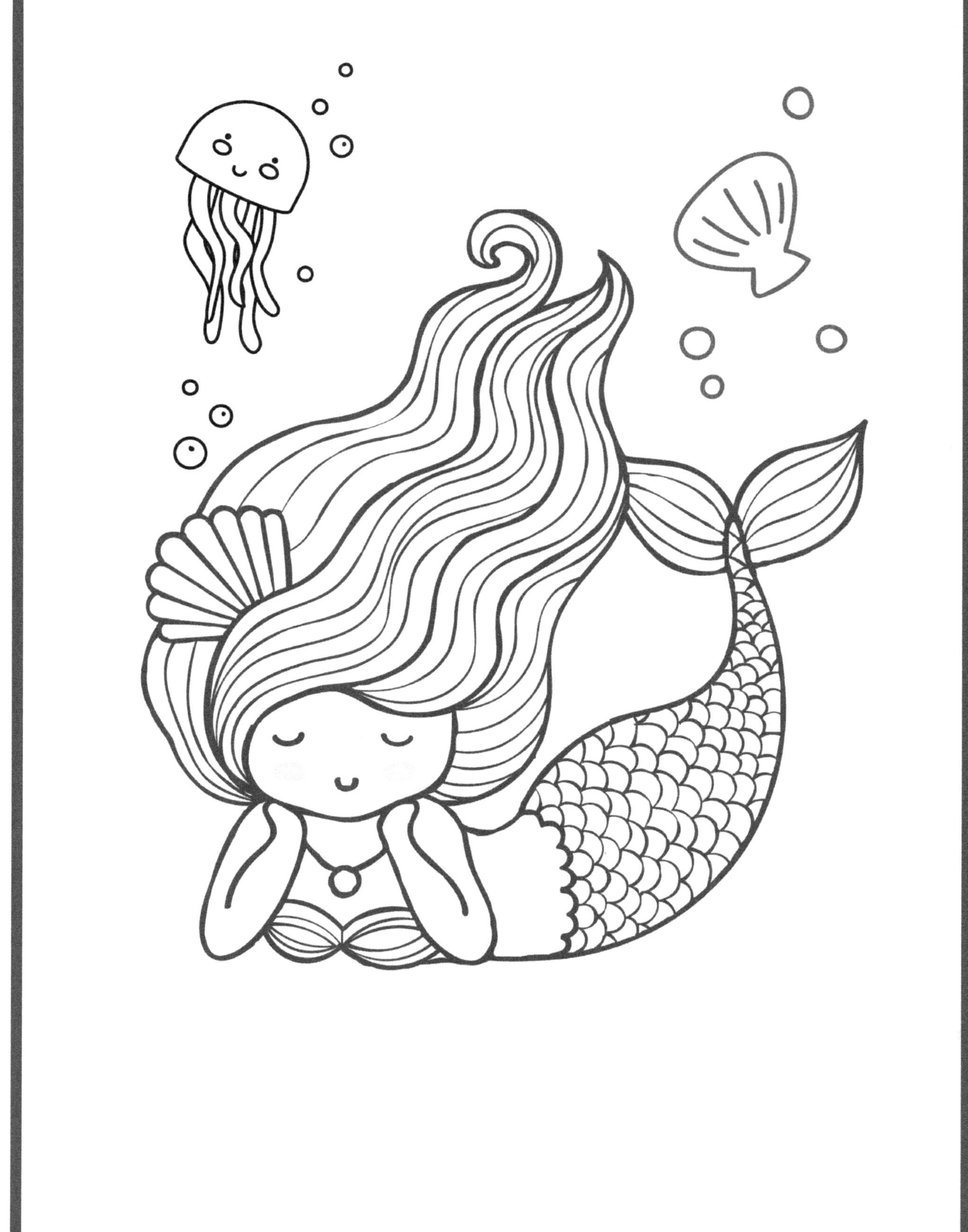

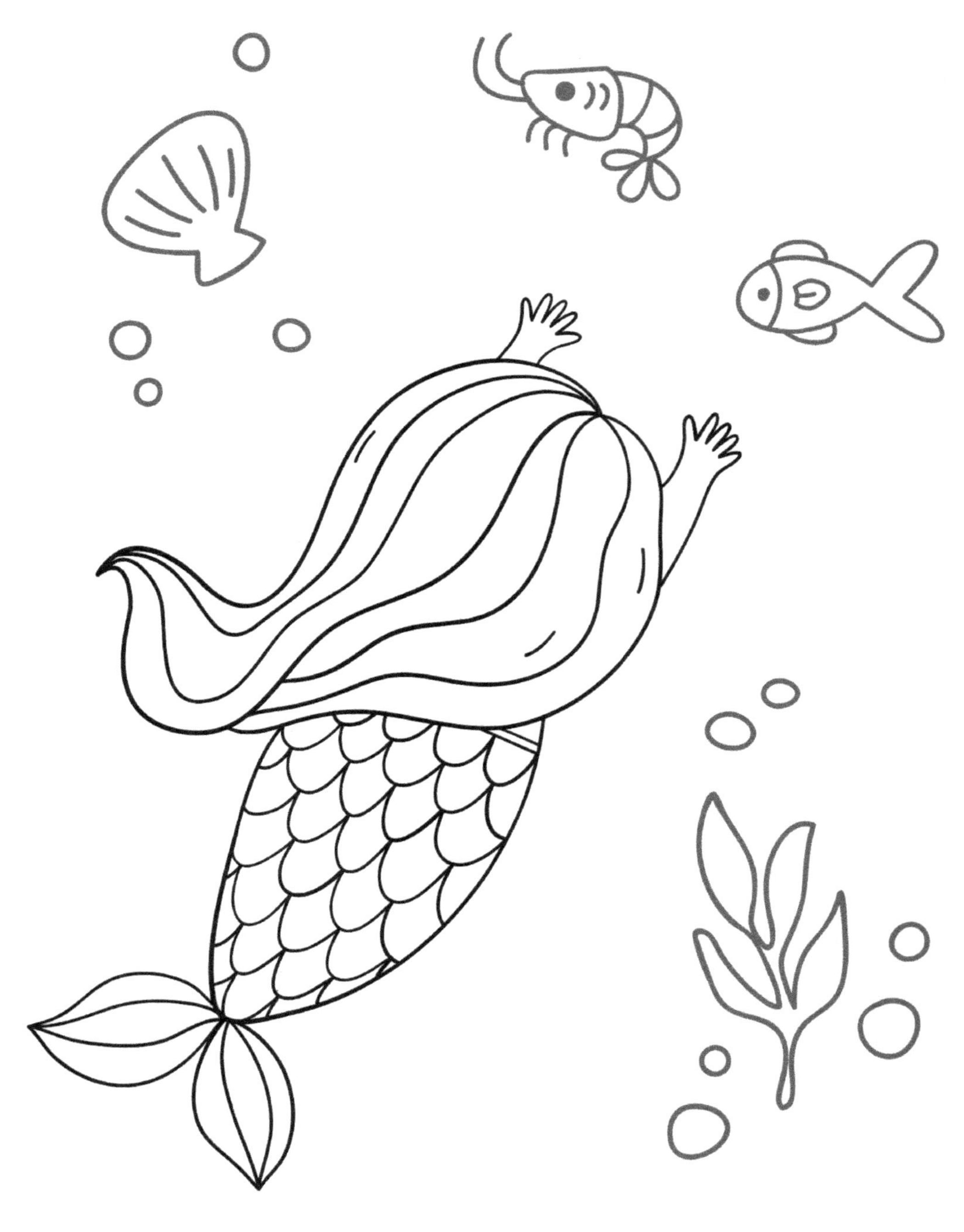

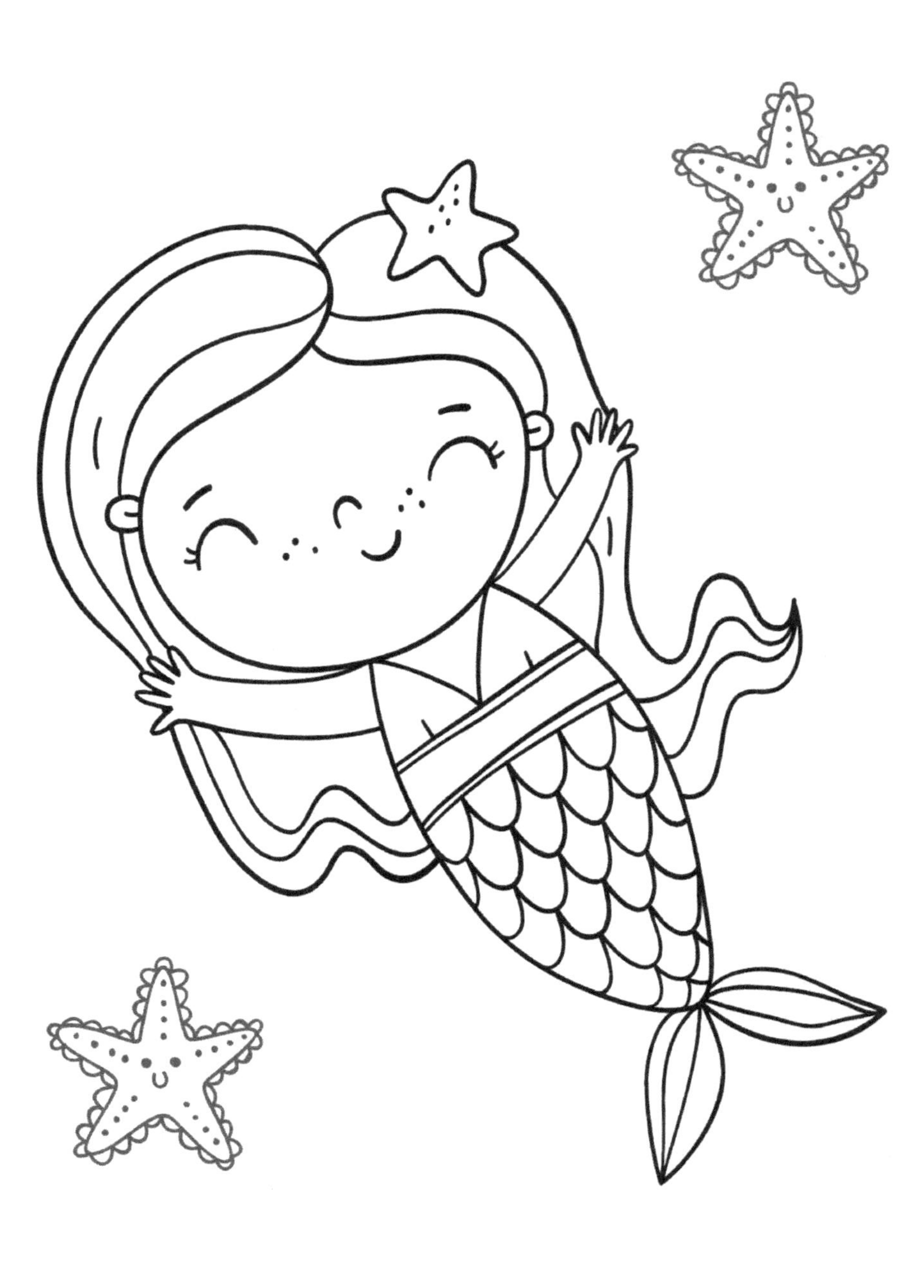

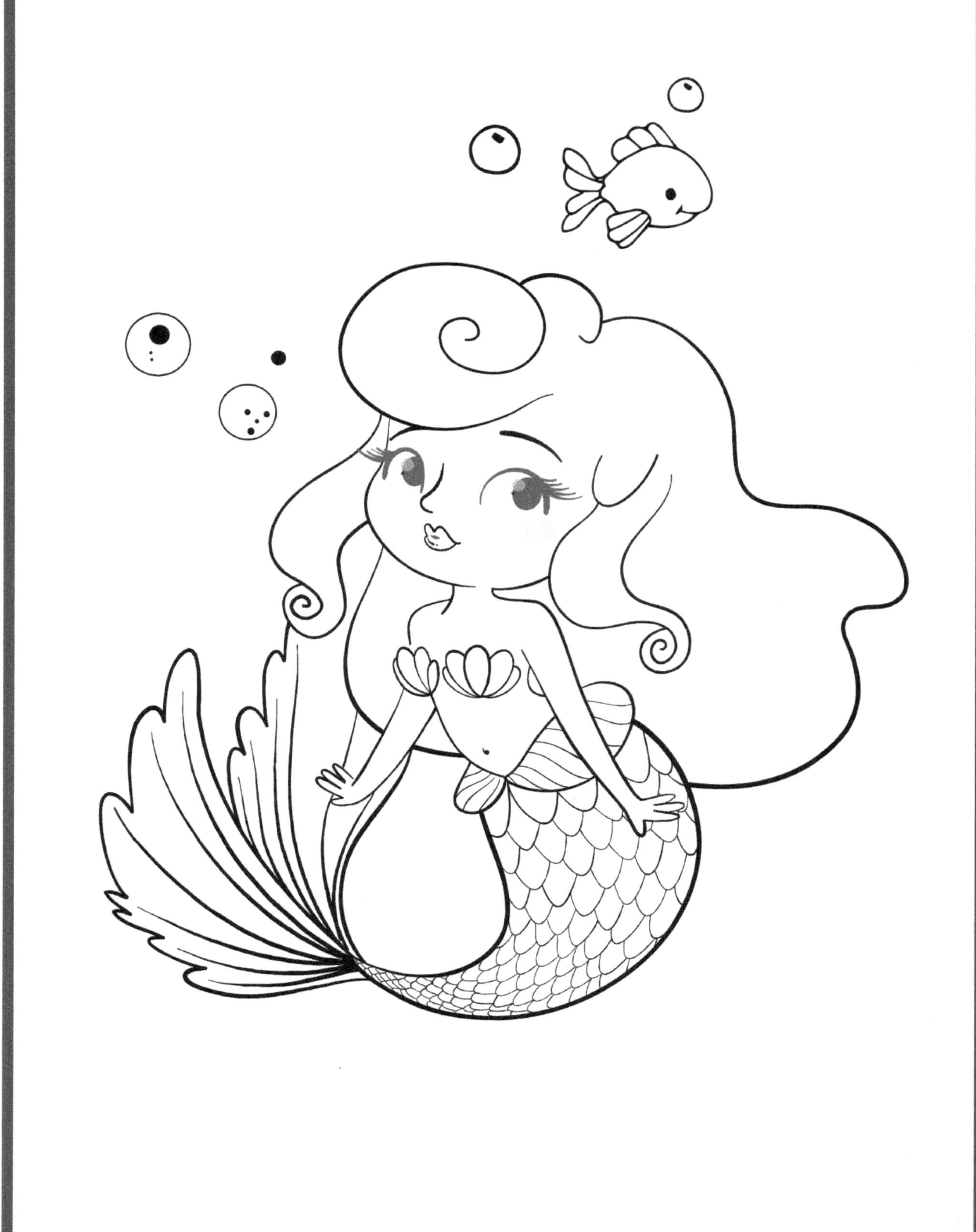

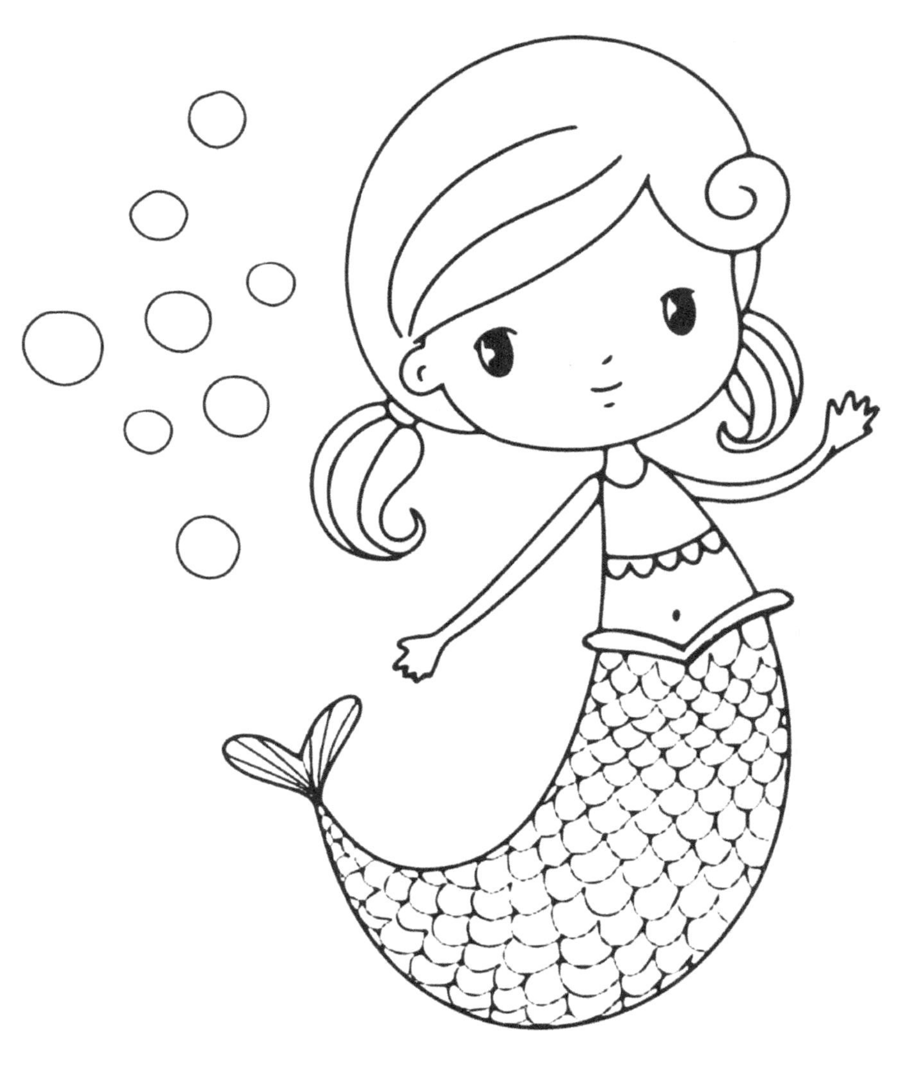